Climbing

Higher

on the

Mystical

Path

Climbing

Higher

on the

Mystical

Path

KIM MICHAELS

MORE TO LIFE PUBLISHING

www.morepublish.com

For foreign and translation rights,

contact info@ morepublish.com

ISBN: 978-9949-518-27-2

Series ISBN: 978-9949-518-21-0

The information and insights in this book should not be considered as a form of therapy, advice, direction, diagnosis, and/or treatment of any kind. This information is not a substitute for medical, psychological, or other professional advice, counseling and care. All matters pertaining to your individual health should be supervised by a physician or appropriate health-care practitioner. No guarantee is made by the author or the publisher that the practices described in this book will yield successful results for anyone at any time. They are presented for informational purposes only, as the practice and proof rests with the individual.

For more information: *www.askrealjesus.com.*

CONTENTS

INTRODUCTION

This book is part of the *From the Heart of Jesus* series, which means the content is given through a process of direct revelation by the ascended master Jesus. For more information on how Jesus brings forth these teachings, see the first book in this series, *The Mystical Teachings of Jesus* or the websites *www.ascendedmasterlight.com* and *www.askrealjesus.com*.

Most of the material in this book was originally published in a book named *Save Yourself*. About 75% of that book is now published in a volume called *Walking the Mystical Path of Jesus*. The remaining 25% are contained in this book. This book also contains quite a bit of material that was originally published as questions and answers on the website *www.ascendedmasteranswers.com*.

1 | WHAT THE MYSTICAL PATH IS ALL ABOUT

Kim: There seems to be a fine balance between focusing on yourself because you want to make spiritual progress and focusing on yourself in a way that can easily morph into a negative self-centeredness. I mean, many people accuse us spiritual seekers of being narcissists.

Jesus: You cannot give a spiritual teaching that cannot be misinterpreted by the dualistic state of consciousness. That is why, again and again, we stress the Middle Way, we stress balance, we stress going beyond duality.

Truly, the key to resolving this is to realize that the path is a state of constant self-observation where you are constantly observing yourself and watching whether you are staying on the Middle Way or whether you have gone into one of the dualistic extremes. Certainly, this is not something that you can give a hard and fast rule and say: "This is what you should always be looking for." One of the things you must understand as mature spiritual seekers is that the path is subtle—and that the further you go along the path, the more subtle it becomes. When you look at someone who is a mass murderer, you can easily see that the person is not on the spiritual path and is doing something clearly nonspiritual. But as you go beyond that level of the blatant outer abuse, it becomes more difficult to discern the delicate difference between going into one of the dualistic extremes. This is where, as you mature, you realize that you need to go beyond what I have called black-and-white thinking and gray thinking. You need to be constantly alert to whether you are being pulled into one extreme or another.

This requires constant alertness, constant self-observation. But I must tell you that there can come a point where you become non-attached to protecting your ego, protecting whatever sense you have of being in control or feeling that you are on the right track. You can come to a point where you are willing to look at anything in your own psychology, and you do not resist seeing the truth. Because you know, as we have said many times, that the Conscious You is more than the outer personality, than the dualistic self. Once you see something as dualistic, you can let it go and you will be freer than you were before.

It is indeed true that there is a stage on the spiritual path where you need to focus first of all on yourself, discovering that beam in your own eye, removing it so that you can attain some sense of inner peace and clarity. Until you have truly helped yourself, how can you possibly help others? Once you have attained some sense of peace, then you come to a point on the path where you cannot progress further until you help other people or help the planet as a whole.

Even this can become a blind alley that can be used by the ego. We have indeed seen some of our more mature students who have fallen into the trap of now focusing on saving the world, or helping other people, or spreading the teachings, or working in a certain spiritual organization, to the point where they have said: "I no longer need to look at my own psychology. Surely, I have gone beyond that need. I have realized what I need to realize on the spiritual path."

Again, there is no one way to always do the right thing. There is no outer rule that can be given. The way to do the right thing is to realize that as long as you are in physical embodiment, you need to reach for a higher understanding of yourself and the spiritual path, you need to be willing to self-transcend.

In a sense the short answer is: No matter what state of consciousness you are in right now, always look for the next level. Always seek to transcend. Observe yourself, and then follow the inner direction when you suddenly encounter an outer situation where you get the inner prompting that here is something you need to look at, here is something to let go of.

This is what all true seekers are doing constantly. As long as you are in physical embodiment, you need to self-transcend. It is only those who continue to self-transcend who will eventually reach that level of self-transcendence where they permanently transcend the material realm.

What I hear you say, and what I know from my own experience, is that the path is not easy. I have never personally found that it involves suffering, but I have nevertheless met spiritual seekers who insist that you cannot make progress without suffering, what is your comment on that?

Suffering is not necessary because suffering comes from attachment. What makes it difficult to walk the path is your attachments. In a sense you could – if you were willing to let go of your attachments – walk the path without any suffering whatsoever.

When we say the path is not easy and that you should not expect it to be easy, it is because we are practical realists who realize – from our own experience – that it is almost impossible to let go of everything at once. We all had to follow a gradual path. We all had to walk step by step and give up certain limitations one at a time so as to preserve some sense of continuity.

The difficulties on the path come from your inability – or in some case unwillingness – to see what you need to see in order to let go of a particular illusion. We know – again from our own experience – that it is difficult to see what you cannot see. This is no different for many of you than it was for myself when I was in embodiment. When you are in embodiment, you are inside your current mental box. It is always difficult to look at your own situation from outside that box. That, incidentally, is why you need guidance from spiritual teachers, from other people and from spiritual teachings.

You can literally come to a state of surrender where even though there are difficult phases of your path, they do not cause you suffering. The physical octave, the material realm, is dense. It is not easy to walk the spiritual path in the density of the collective consciousness. When you reach a certain state of surrender, the difficulties you encounter will not cause you suffering. The reason is that you have surrendered your expectations, you have surrendered your conditions.

There are many people who find the spiritual path and they realize that in order to walk the path they have to make what they see as sacrifices. Because they have to give up some of their old lifestyle, some of the activities in which the world indulges, such as alcohol, drugs, material pursuits and many other things that take you away from the spiritual path. People get enthusiastic and they are willing to give up some of these activities. But they still feel that they have made a sacrifice in doing so. Their egos trick them into building the subtle expectation that when they have sacrificed for the path or sacrificed for God, then after that point everything should be easy. God should simply pave the way for them so that they do not encounter any more challenges or difficulties.

This, of course, is the ego trying to trick people into building an unrealistic expectation that is guaranteed to cause disappointment so that they become discouraged and stop walking the path. Or they get angry, as some people do, feeling that they were given empty promises by a particular organization or teacher. Their egos trick them into abandoning the path.

When you give up your conditions, you have no expectations of what the path should be like. How can anything that occurs to you cause you suffering. Suffering is caused by a psychological condition that causes you to emotionally and mentally rebel against what you are experiencing in the physical world.

You will see that many people who have encountered great physical difficulties have come to a state of surrender and peace where they have accepted the condition and accepted that they can – no matter how difficult the outer conditions are – make the best of it and still have a joyful life. Look at some of the people who have physical handicaps, such as sitting in a wheelchair. Many of the people who experience this become depressed, but there are a few who rise above it and become joyful and are at peace with the situation, making the best of it.

Suffering is not caused by the outer condition but by the inner psychological condition of rebelling against the outer physical condition. That is why, when you are on the spiritual path, you would do well to give up your outer conditions and expectations of what the path should be like. You should know, as spiritual people, that the physical realm is dense, that the collective consciousness is dense. You should not expect it to be easy and trouble-free to walk the path.

You certainly should not either go into the opposite extreme of thinking that in order to be spiritual, you have to suffer—and walk up a mountain barefoot because somehow that pays for your sins because God is pleased the more you suffer. The more you suffer the more sins he will forgive.

Again, there is the Middle Way. When you find the Middle Way, you can overcome all difficulties and maintain the joy. When you decide to meet all difficulties with joy and you are willing to transcend, then the difficulties are not so difficult. They are simply events in the physical realm. You move beyond them because you have a clear vision of your goal.

You know where you want to go and it is not a matter of thinking that you can only go there if there are no obstacles. You know there will be obstacles and that it is simply a matter of overcoming them, moving beyond them, rising above them, walking right through them—so that you find the joyous path that is independent of the outer conditions because your joy is full.

I have met many people who build up a certain frustration as they walk the path. Some feel that every answer they get only generates a dozen more questions. I have met people who feel like they are working on a complex jigsaw puzzle and every time they manage to fit one piece into the puzzle, a whole new load of pieces is dumped on the table. How can people avoid such frustration?

I fully understand the feeling that every time you think you have found one answer that answer leads to more questions. However, what such people are going through is only a temporary phase, and as they grow toward Christhood, it will come to an end.

When you start the spiritual path, it is like trying to assemble a jigsaw puzzle without having the box. You don't know what the assembled puzzle is supposed to look like so how can you tell where a piece is supposed to fit? As you continue to study spiritual teachings and seek intuitive insights, you will one day be able to see the picture on the jigsaw puzzle even though some of the pieces might still be missing. These qualities are needed for spiritual seekers on the path:

- You are willing to consider a topic even though it is difficult and goes beyond your current knowledge and beliefs.

- You are willing to wrestle with the difficult questions and you refuse to let them go until you find a higher understanding.

Even if people sometimes walk away from the table, this is part of the process. You cannot resolve some of these deep questions with the outer, analytical mind. Once you have stimulated creative tension, it is necessary to walk away and give your outer mind a rest so that the answer can surface through intuitive insights. The entire process is the process of discovering and applying the key of knowledge. You might recall that I said the lawyers had taken away the key of knowledge: "Woe unto you, lawyers! for ye have taken away the key of knowledge: ye entered not in yourselves, and them that were entering in ye hindered." (Luke 11:52)

The lawyers believed, as do many orthodox Christians today, that the truth can be found only in the outer scriptures, in the letter of the law. They were not willing to go beyond the outer scriptures and doctrines in order to achieve an intuitive understanding. They wanted only to consider what could be described in words and what could be interpreted literally. The simple fact is that words are linear, and the spiritual reality is spherical. There is a limitation that makes it impossible to fully describe the spiritual reality with words. This becomes even more of a problem when people have descended into the dualistic state of consciousness that takes linear words and makes them relative on top of being linear. This makes it very difficult to explain spiritual truth by using words because people will often interpret those words according to what they want to believe.

The only way for spiritual seekers to know truth is to use words, such as an outer scripture or the words I give in this book, only as a stepping stone. The fallacy of so many orthodox religious people is that they believe the truth about God can be confined to a scripture composed of words. In reality, no scripture was ever released for the purpose of giving a complete and infallible description of the spiritual reality. It is intended to give people a foundation that they could stand on as they reach beyond the outer words and open their minds to an intuitive experience that goes beyond words. The words are only meant to be a tool that enables the mind to reach beyond the material universe and receive an insight that cannot be expressed in words.

This is the key to overcoming frustration. As people continue walking the path and using the many tools we have given, they will gradually become more attuned to their Christ selves. Thereby, they will receive more profound insights about the spiritual reality. Many of those insights will be inner experiences that are in many dimensions, almost like the difference between watching a photograph and experiencing the actual object in three dimensions. Some of these experiences simply cannot be expressed in words, yet they will still unlock your understanding of who you are. These direct inner experiences will gradually take you beyond the stage of feeling frustrated and bewildered. The confusing array of questions will give way to inner experiences that generate knowing.

> **How about humor? I have over the years met many, many spiritual seekers who take themselves and the spiritual path very seriously, almost as if the fate of the world hangs on their shoulders. Is it not a kind of soul disease to take your path too seriously? Is there any room for humor in the spiritual realm?**

I can assure you that there is much humor and joy here in the spiritual realm, and there should be room for humor on the spiritual path on earth. Let me say that if you cannot laugh at yourself, you are taking yourself too seriously. If you cannot laugh at a particular topic, including your religion, you are taking that topic too seriously.

Humor is indeed a liberating force that can have a powerful impact on setting people free from the prison of the human ego and the dualistic mind. The human ego is very serious about preserving its image and its sense of being in control. When you identify with the ego, you cannot laugh at yourself. If you think someone is making fun of you, the ego feels threatened, and it attempts to squeeze all joy from your life. One of the best ways to neutralize the ego is to use humor.

As Saint Thomas More once said: "The devil, the evil spirit, cannot endure to be mocked." There is indeed no better way to turn away dark forces than by using humor. The dark forces are consumed by their egos, and they take themselves very seriously—and they want all human beings to do the same. If you refuse to take them seriously, or even use humor to deflate their egos, they will find it difficult to find an inroad into your consciousness.

Obviously, as with everything else on this planet, there is a higher form of humor and a lower form of humor. I am sure everyone interested in spiritual growth can tell the difference, and it is truly a difference in vibration. Some forms of humor are gross or base, and they cause your energies to flow downward. Other forms of humor are light-hearted and cause your energies to move up. I am not encouraging anyone to engage in any lower form of humor, which is basically any form of humor that degrades other human beings. However, I strongly encourage people to use humor as part of the spiritual path because it truly can liberate you from becoming trapped in the illusion created by dark forces, namely that everything is so serious and should be taken so seriously that there is no room for any real joy in life.

Many Christians have developed the attitude that it is necessary to walk around with a sad face in order to make it to heaven. In reality, this is an illusion. God has no desire to force people to enter heaven. God wants people to enter of their own free-will choosing, and why would you choose to enter heaven if you see it as a place with no joy?

God created human beings so they are naturally attracted to that which is light and joyful, and they are repulsed by that which is dark and dreary. God created you that way because heaven is full of light and joy, and God wants you to be attracted to heaven. If your religion makes you take life too seriously, then you are not headed in the direction of heaven. If not, you might want to lighten up and take your spirituality and your religion less seriously. It is quite possible to laugh your way into heaven but it is not possible to cry your way into heaven.

We of the ascended masters often use humor to diffuse a tense situation. Although heaven is a place with great joy, those of us working with human beings often find ourselves in somewhat tense situations because it is difficult to determine exactly how to help our unascended brothers and sisters move forward on the spiritual path. Truly, there are so many problems and so much darkness in the earth that even an ascended master can become tense when dealing with these situations. We often used humor to lighten a meeting or discussion because we know that when things get too tense, the tension itself will block the right solution.

Up here, we never make fun of people or each other in a malicious or degrading way. But we will make fun of each other in a good-natured way, and we will make fun of ourselves because we do not take ourselves too seriously. We will often use our past mistakes or shortcomings in a humorous way to prove a point. If you want an example of our form of humor, read *The Jesus Koans*. It contains some sayings that bring a smile to the face of an ascended being.

Let me say that humor and joy is truly a vibration. It is a vibration of great light, and it can lift your spirit more than anything else. Humor is not necessarily the same as laughter. Laughter is a physiological reaction, and although it can relax your muscles, it does not necessarily lift your spirit. Base humor does not lift your spirit.

It is quite possible to use humor and joy without making people laugh. Joy can be a quiet glow that suddenly makes everyone realize that behind all the serious appearances on earth there is a deeper sense of joy. That joy can be released through the heart center of every human being, but those who are truly joyful can become electrodes of this inner glow. They can lighten up a room simply by walking into it and without cracking any jokes that make people laugh. They can open the door for a flood tide of the energy of joy simply by looking at someone with a blink in the eye or by smiling. As you grow on the spiritual path, heal your psychological wounds and open your mind and heart to spiritual light, you will naturally become an electrode of joy. You will be able to dispel the gloom of a situation by just being the flame of joy in action.

Many Christians have an impression of me as being quiet and reserved. I do not know where that impression came from because if you read the scriptures, you will see that I was not quiet or reserved when I challenged the scribes and the Pharisees. I was, and I am, a very direct Master, and I can assure you that I was quite outspoken. Many people were offended by my outspokenness and directness. It is, however, correct that I did not often smile or laugh during my embodiment in Galilee. I knew I had a serious mission to fulfill, and from the point of no return at the wedding in Cana, I was so focused on meeting the daily tests and challenges that I had little attention left over for being joyful.

In retrospect, I wish I had been more joyful but at the time my attention was focused on dealing with the heavy energies and the outer challenges I faced. Today, I would have been far less serious but then again it is easy to look back at the past and think you could have done better.

Nevertheless, I see no reason people today should take themselves, their religion or the spiritual side of life too seriously. Make an effort to bring joy into your spiritual life because unless you become as joyful as little children, how can you enter the kingdom of joy? Make an effort to become an electrode of joy and dispel the cloud of gloom that currently hangs over this planet. Many people in today's world take themselves and their causes so seriously that they believe joyfulness is a sin, a crime or an offense to God. I can assure you that God is never offended by true joy. On the contrary, God is the most joyful being you will ever meet. How can there be anything but joy in the Presence of God?

2 | HOW TO TRULY LEARN FROM A SPIRITUAL MASTER

Some people find teachings on the websites or in the books that immediately ring true in their hearts. They find other ideas that are so far beyond or contradict the religious doctrines they were taught in childhood that they find it difficult to accept these ideas. How would you recommend people respond to that?

It is the truth that will set you free. If you currently had the truth, you would already be free. In order to give you the truth, I have to contradict the erroneous beliefs you currently have. Contradicting people's current beliefs has always been the role of a true spiritual master, and it will always be so. That is why a master can help only those who are willing to have their cherished beliefs contradicted.

Many people recognize that there is truth in our teachings. However, they also find specific teachings that they cannot currently accept. If this applies to you, I can assure you that you are not alone in this experience. The question now becomes how you deal with this situation?

Let me ask you to consider the situation from my perspective. I have brought forth these teachings for the specific purpose of helping people attain a higher understanding. The ultimate goal is to inspire people to anchor themselves on the spiritual path that will gradually lead them to the full Christ consciousness that I demonstrated 2,000 years ago.

As I explain in the previous books, most people on this planet are trapped in a lower state of consciousness in which many of their beliefs and viewpoints are affected or dominated by relative ideas that spring from the dualistic mind. Most people have been brought up with a set of beliefs and ideas that are out of alignment with the truth and the reality of God. This has caused most people to build a sense of identity as being limited, mortal human beings. This sense of identity is out of alignment with the reality of God, namely that every lifestream is a spiritual being with the potential to win immortal life through the Christ consciousness.

My role as a spiritual master is to help people go through a transformation in consciousness. This is first and foremost a transformation of people's sense of identity so that they grow out of the limited sense of identity as being mortal human beings and gradually come to accept a new sense of identity as being immortal spiritual beings. This then is the goal. Everything in our teachings is designed to help the greatest possible number of people attain that growth, that transformation of identity.

Take note of the basic mechanism involved. To attain a true sense of identity, you must let go of the limited sense of identity you currently have. This means that you must let go of the ideas and beliefs that make up your limited sense of identity. How can I help you change your sense of identity? I must help you see beyond the limited beliefs that make up your current sense of identity. To do that, I must speak the truth, even if it is in opposition to your current beliefs.

I cannot help you build a true sense of identity by affirming beliefs that are out of alignment with the truth and the reality of God. This simply is not possible. If you are to become a Christed being, you must let go of every aspect of your sense of identity that is out of alignment with the truth of God. There are no exceptions to this. It is not possible to take a false belief with you into the kingdom of heaven. That is why I said that he who is willing to lose his life – meaning his mortal sense of identity – for my sake – for the sake of attaining Christ consciousness – shall find it, meaning that he or she shall find immortal life in the Christ consciousness.

I now ask you to consider that our websites are available to every human being on this planet with access to a computer. If you take a quick look at humanity, it should not be difficult to see that people are at many different levels of consciousness. Many of the people who find the websites do not have the same background or the same beliefs that you have. Our teachings are not made specifically for you or for people who share your background and your beliefs. I am attempting to reach out to the greatest possible number of people, and I am simply asking you to respect the fact that in order to reach the greatest number of people I cannot tailor the teachings to your personal beliefs or what makes you feel comfortable.

I am not asking you to agree with everything in this book. I am asking you to respect the fact that what might seem uncomfortable or offensive to you could still be at teaching that will help another lifestream let go of an illusion and rise to a higher level on the spiritual path. Should I abstain from helping that other lifestream in order to avoid making you feel uncomfortable, or are you willing to let me speak the truth that will help another, even if it does make you feel uncomfortable?

Now let me take this to another level. It should not be difficult to see that I seek to inspire people to anchor themselves on the spiritual path that leads you from your current state of consciousness to the Christ consciousness. I consistently portray this as a gradual path that consists of many stages and many individual steps. This is most clearly expressed in my discourse on the levels of spiritual development given in the previous book. [*Walking the Mystical Path of Jesus*]

The people who find our teachings are at different levels of the spiritual path. Right now, you are at a particular level on your personal path. You are facing certain tests, certain initiations, and to pass them you need a certain spiritual teaching. Once you go beyond this level, you will face other tests and other initiations and you will need a higher teaching. This is compatible to what you see in the educational systems of the world. You do not teach advanced algebra to students in kindergarten. You take a gradual approach, and a kindergarten student is not ready to deal with the knowledge that will be released at the college level.

I am trying to release teachings for a broad range of students. I realize that there are many people in the world, especially many mainstream Christians, who will not be able to accept the basic idea behind the teachings or many of the individual teachings. They are simply not at a level of their personal path where I can reach them through these teachings. I also realize that there are certain students who have passed beyond the teachings I am releasing here. I am not trying to reach everyone, but I am trying to reach a relatively broad spectrum. There are certain teachings that some people might not be ready for. The consequence is that many people find some teachings that ring true in their hearts but they find other teachings that they simply cannot deal with at their current level of consciousness. Once again, how do you handle that situation?

The most immature response is that people take the one teaching that they cannot deal with and use it as an excuse for rejecting everything else. Many orthodox Christians, especially fundamentalist Christians, immediately fall into this pattern when they find our websites.

A much more mature response is to realize that at your current level of the spiritual path, you don't have to deal with that particular teaching. You don't need to make a decision with your outer mind concerning whether you should accept or reject the teaching. Instead, you can decide not to make a decision about the teaching. You can put it on the shelf and continue to walk your personal path until at some future time you feel an inner prompting to take the teaching off the shelf.

This is a perfectly legitimate approach. You recognize the fact that the spiritual path is a gradual process and that there are ideas that you don't need to deal with at your current level. You put them on the shelf until some future time when you are ready. While this is a valid approach, it is only legitimate up to a point. You need to be aware that there is a fine line between putting something on the shelf and going into denial about the necessity to consider the teaching.

If you are in the third grade, you can go into the school library and find a book on math for the senior year of high school. Obviously, you are not ready to read that book. Nevertheless, if you get to senior year of high school and still refuse to read the book, then you will limit your education and possibly flunk the exam.

I encourage you to continue to study the teachings that you can deal with. If you cannot currently deal with my teachings on a particular topic, then it might be legitimate for you to put them aside for now. Be aware of the fact that at some point in the future you will need to consider them again.

Let me also mention that my teachings are meant to inspire people to close the circle and enter into a more direct relationship with me as their spiritual master. This is an inner relationship where you work with me independently of the outer teaching. The main requirement for entering this personal relationship is that you must come to a point where you are willing to consider my teachings even if they go beyond or contradict your current beliefs. If you are not willing to let me challenge your current beliefs, you are not ready for this closer relationship.

It is perfectly acceptable for you to come to the teachings and "cherry-pick," meaning that you study the teachings that appeal to you and ignore others. If you desire a closer personal relationship with me, you must be willing to let me challenge any of your current beliefs. I am not hereby saying that you have to let go of all of your current beliefs. I am saying you must *be willing* to let go of any of those beliefs as you get direction from within. If you have a belief that you are not willing to have challenged, then you are simply not ready for this personal relationship with me. I will then patiently wait until you are ready, but be aware that no lifestream has forever to come home.

My goal for these teachings is to help lifestreams grow. In order to help you grow, I must help you abandon your incorrect or incomplete beliefs. If you feel emotionally attached to some of those beliefs, then I might have to challenge your beliefs even if it makes you feel uncomfortable. My goal for the teachings is not to make you feel comfortable. My goal is to help you grow. If this requires me to challenge your beliefs and make you feel uncomfortable for a time, then I am perfectly willing to do that, as I was perfectly willing to challenge the scribes and the Pharisees 2,000 years ago.

I once had a person say that all of the books should be made available online for free like the rest of the teachings on the websites. He even implied that if we are selling anything it discredits you as being a genuine spiritual teacher.

There are many people who find the websites and are deeply disturbed by the possibility that I, the real Jesus Christ, could actually be speaking through someone and putting my inner teachings on a website that is available to all. They are disturbed by this because they have created an image of me that makes them feel they have me and my teachings under control. They are disturbed by the possibility that I cannot be controlled because I can speak through people who choose to tune in to me and be the open door for the Living Word. When such people find the websites, they are, consciously or subconsciously, looking for anything that will give them an excuse for rejecting my teachings.

There is a spiritual reason why not all of the books are available for free. To understand that reason, you need to understand the basic spiritual law that guides the interchange between a spiritual master and the students of that master. This law basically states that the master is allowed to offer the student a certain amount of teaching for free, meaning that the student can receive that teaching without giving anything in return. When I say giving something in return, I first of all mean that the student makes a commitment to embody and apply the teaching and to follow the master.

The Bible tells people to freely give what they have freely received. The master gives freely to the student, and in an ideal situation the student will multiply the gift and give part of it back to the master. When the master gives to the student, it is like one half of a circle. Spiritual teachings and spiritual energy flows from the master to the student. If the student takes the spiritual teaching and does not make a commitment to the master, then the circle will remain open. Only when the student makes a commitment and applies the teaching, will the circle be closed. Only when the circle is closed can the master release more light and teaching to the student.

When the circle is closed, a figure-eight flow is established between the master and the student. The light of the master flows to the student who then multiplies that light and sends it back to the master. The master can then multiply the offering from the student and give the student more light and teaching. This becomes a self-reinforcing spiral that will gradually lift the student to a higher level of consciousness, the level of consciousness attained by the master.

However, for the circle to be complete, the student must give something back to the master. This is what is expressed in the law of the tithe where people give a part of their income to God so that God has something to multiply and give back to them. This law was created after the Fall of Man, and it says that a spiritual master cannot continue to give to a student unless the student multiplies the first offering. The master is allowed to give the student an initial gift. Unless the student multiplies the initial offering, the master is not allowed to give any more to that student.

The law is explained in great detail in my parable about the talents. You will notice that both of the servants who had multiplied the talents received more in return. The servant who had buried his talents in the ground, and thereby refused to multiply them, could receive no more and therefore lost everything. You might also consider the situation where I multiplied the loaves and the fishes in order to feed the multitudes. Why did I not simply manifest food? Because the law would not allow me to do so. The law states that I was allowed to multiply what the students had brought to the altar of God. They have brought loaves and fishes, and that is why I multiplied them manifold. Had they brought nothing, there would have been nothing for me to multiply and the multitudes would not have been fed.

When you understand this spiritual law, you realize that the websites represents the initial offering that I, as the spiritual master, give to the students, meaning those who find the websites. It is my desire to close the circle between myself and anyone who finds this websites and who is willing to enter at master-student relationship with me. For the closing of the circle to occur, the student must multiply my initial offering and give something back to me.

The multiplication of the offering first of all means that the student must internalize the teaching and make a commitment to raising his or her consciousness. This has nothing to do with any outer physical action and is certainly not dependent on the person supporting the websites in any physical way. There are levels of commitment and the greater the commitment from the student the greater the multiplication from me.

One level of commitment is that the student takes the teachings seriously, studies them, applies them and allows them to transform his or her understanding and consciousness. At some point the student should also take some outer action as a result of internalizing the teachings. One such action could be to use the spiritual techniques that we offer on the toolbox website. This includes the decrees for spiritual protection, the calls for the transformation of negative energy on a personal and planetary scale and the beautiful rosaries and invocations released by Mother Mary. By giving such spiritual exercises, the student will make a contribution to the purification of the consciousness of humankind and the energy field of the entire planet. This then will allow me to give more light back to the student and establish the figure-eight flow. Another way for the student to complete the circle is to spread the word about the teachings or to tell other people about the insights they have garnered from them. Students can help me spread my inner teachings. Finally, a student can also take the physical action of supporting the websites financially. The books are a convenient way for people to support the websites.

While the Internet is a great tool, it also has limitations. One is that so many people expect to get something for free without giving anything in return. Another is that reading a spiritual teaching piece by piece (often in a random order) is not the same as reading a book where you get a teaching that builds a more sequential progression. You will get a more profound experience from reading the teachings in a book. If someone finds something of value on the websites, there should come a point where the person wants to read one of the books.

The underlying purpose of the teachings is to give people a bridge whereby they can establish a master-student relationship directly with me or another ascended master. The key to establishing this relationship is to make a commitment and to multiply the teachings that I have freely given on the websites. As I said, the law only allows me to multiply that which the student places on the altar. I can do nothing beyond what the law allows me to do, and it is truly up to the student to close the circle and establish the figure-eight flow between us.

Some people say that your teachings are very direct, even stern. They say a true ascended master would never speak in such a way and that masters are always kind and loving. Do you have a response to that?

There is a very important turning point on the path when you begin to take responsibility for yourself and become willing to change yourself. At the beginning stages of this process, people still have some insecurity so they look for spiritual teachings that make them feel good, tell them what they want to hear and don't challenge their existing beliefs too much. This is natural, and I am not blaming people for this reaction. However, there is a limit to how much you can grow as long as you maintain this approach.

There is also a real danger that you will take a time-consuming detour into the gray thinking described in the books on the ego. The process is simple. When you rise above black-and-white thinking, you will be confronted with the temptation to engage in gray thinking. Since you no longer believe in an infallible authority, the ego will seek to make you believe that no messenger or channeler is completely objective and reliable. It really doesn't matter which one you follow so you might as well follow one you like. However, for many people this means they end up following a messenger their egos like because the teachings do not challenge the ego. What the ego is really saying is that you should accept no authority as being above the ego, and you should ignore any teacher or teaching that challenges your ego's pet theories. If you fall into this trap, how will you ever see through the illusions of the ego?

When you become a more mature seeker, you realize the fundamental mechanism behind all true channeling/messages. The simple fact is that the ascended masters have a higher state of consciousness than you do. Your advantage of studying our teachings is that we can help you see what you cannot see and what your ego does not want you to see. We can tell you what your ego does not want you to hear and what students who still identify with their egos do not want to hear.

It is an eternal fact that immature and insecure students seek out messages that tell them what they want to hear and never challenge their most cherished beliefs. In contrast, mature students deliberately seek out teachings that do challenge their most cherished beliefs. As you mature, you realize that the real value of the ascended masters' teachings is that they do challenge your beliefs, compelling you to reach beyond the ego's dualistic understanding. This is simply the only way you will come up higher.

When I talk about challenging your beliefs, I am not simply talking about the words spoken and the teachings given. I am talking about a more general approach. Some gurus are very stern and direct and openly and often harshly challenge their students and mercilessly point out flaws in their beliefs, attitude and behavior. This is simply one way, and the way of other gurus is to be much more gentle, soft-spoken and more patient with their disciples, preferring them to discover their own flaws rather than pointing them out. One method is not generally better or more efficient than another, as each method works best for certain levels of consciousness.

There is a large number of spiritual seekers who are naturally very loving, kind and gentle people. Such students will naturally prefer the gentle type of guru and will generally shun the direct type of guru, fearing to be hurt by his sternness. In reality, the more gentle people need a stern guru. The reason is that you will make the fastest progress by selecting a guru that is the opposite of your own type, for this will give you more balance in your own being. If you are a gentle person, you need to reach a point where you are not in the least bothered by a direct guru, and if you are the direct type, you need to learn the patience of a gentle guru.

There is a level of consciousness that is prone to gray thinking. This consciousness causes students to interpret spiritual teachings to mean what they want to hear, not being able to free themselves from the dualistic logic of the ego. I can assure you that such students are very difficult to reach, for some of them truly think they know better than the ascended masters, even better than God, which is why they descended to earth in the first place and have not risen above it.

When evaluating a spiritual teaching, be very careful that you do not project your own beliefs and opinions upon the teaching or the spiritual master who gives it. A message can be affected by the mind of the messenger, but the mind of the student can also affect how the message is interpreted. Be willing to look for the beam in your own eye, for it is only by removing it that *you* will progress.

Another common pitfall is that some seekers focus on the exact outer form of a given message or a messenger's work, often comparing it to other teachings or what the person wants to believe. This has caused many otherwise open-minded spiritual seekers to become almost fundamentalists with certain new teachings, splitting hairs over whether a particular wording is correct according to this or that standard. Let me tell a little analogy to illustrate this.

Imagine you have grown up in a dark cave. After fumbling your way around for years, you come upon a tube sticking out of the wall. The tube is a kaleidoscope, and as you look into it, you see light streaming through it from outside the cave. As all kaleidoscopes, it has a number of glass pieces inside it so the light is somewhat colored as it passes through. The real significance of your discovery is that it proves beyond any doubt that *there is a world outside your dark cave!* Instead of continuing to look at the light through the kaleidoscope, you can look for the door so you can enter the light yourself.

The fundamental significance of all true spiritual messages is that they demonstrate for those who have eyes to see that there is a higher level of consciousness than the level at which they are trapped. There are spiritual teachers at that level who can communicate with people and help them rise to the ascended consciousness. As I said 2,000 years ago: "God is a Spirit and they that worship him must worship him in spirit and in truth" (John 4:24).

The meaning is that genuine messages from the ascended masters are given from a higher level of consciousness. The outer form of the messages is not nearly as significant as the fact that they come from a higher Spirit. To truly "get the message" we seek to pass on, you must raise your consciousness and make a direct *inner* contact with the Spirit of Truth that we are. If you focus your attention on the outer form of the message, you will not attain that direct experience, and our messages will not set you free. Instead, they will simply be used by your ego to keep you trapped at a certain level of consciousness.

As I explain in my ego discourses, the essential problem on planet earth is that people have descended into a lower state of consciousness in which they are trapped in what the Buddha called Maya, meaning ignorance and illusion. The veil of Maya prevents them from seeing the higher truth of the Christ mind, and instead they can only see the relative "truth" springing from the mind of anti-christ.

The trick here is that people do not realize their beliefs are relative illusions; they believe they are absolutely true and this is why they are still stuck in those beliefs. How can a spiritual teacher help people rise higher? Only by challenging people's illusions so they gradually purify their minds of the illusions and begin to see the truth of Christ. The role of the Living Christ and the true purpose of genuine messages from above is to *challenge people's beliefs*. I stated this clearly 2,000 years ago when I said:

> Think not that I am come to send peace on earth: I
> came not to send peace, but a sword. (Matthew 10:34

> I am come to send fire on the earth; and what will I, if
> it be already kindled? (Luke 12:49)
> For I am come to set a man at variance against his
> father, and the daughter against her mother, and the
> daughter in law against her mother in law. (Matthew
> 10:35)

The deeper meaning is that the greatest threat to people's
spiritual growth is the unwillingness to move, the unwillingness to transcend one's current beliefs. In order to get people
moving, the Living Christ must challenge people's beliefs in
such a provocative way that they simply cannot ignore it, cannot remain indifferent or cannot remain convinced that they
know everything. It is better that people reject our truth than
remain indifferent:

> 15 I know thy works, that thou art neither cold nor
> hot: I would thou wert cold or hot.
> 16 So then because thou art lukewarm, and neither
> cold nor hot, I will spue thee out of my mouth. (Rev-
> elation, Chapter 3)

Take note that there is a subtle truth here which many spiritual seekers have not understood. It is a fact that even a genuine spiritual teaching given by the ascended masters can be
used by the ego to trap people at a certain level of consciousness where people feel they have it all figured out and become
inflexible and unwilling to move higher. It can sometimes be
necessary for the Living Christ to challenge viewpoints that

are technically correct but that people's egos have used to imprison them on a certain level of the path.

We of the ascended masters recognize fully that as soon as a teaching is expressed in words, it enters the realm of duality where it becomes subject to interpretation. People simply project their own state of consciousness upon the teaching and interpret it to mean what their egos want to hear. We have no illusions whatsoever about bringing forth an ultimate teaching that is the infallible word of God, as the fundamentalists claim about the Bible. We often find it necessary to bring forth teachings that deliberately challenge beliefs that imprison large groups of people. We sometimes even have to bring forth a new teaching that challenges the mindset of people who have used a previous teaching to get themselves stuck.

Wise students will recognize that what holds them back on the path is the erroneous beliefs that they believe to be true. Wise students will deliberately seek out teachers or teachings that challenge their existing beliefs, attitude to life and approach to the spiritual path. In contrast, the immature students will look for teachings that affirm what they already believe, "confirming" that they are on the right track—which is exactly what the ego wants them to believe.

The inevitable consequence is that immature students are stuck in either black-and-white or gray thinking. Those who are stuck in gray thinking tend to believe that virtually any teaching is as good as any other teaching so they might as well select the most pleasant one. Many of the students who have matured above black-and-white thinking have become enticed by an incorrect view of love that is floating around in the New Age and even the progressive Christian community. The view says that love is tolerant of everything and never challenges anything. Any teaching which is direct and challenging cannot be from the highest source.

The real consciousness behind both black-and-white and gray thinking is a tendency to believe that you know how the ascended masters should express themselves. This is only a short step away from the consciousness of the fallen angels who are firmly convinced they know better than God how the universe works and how humankind should be saved.

This is a very dangerous place for a spiritual seeker to be. The reason being that even though you have risen above black-and-white thinking, you are still not teachable for a true spiritual teacher. No true teacher will compromise truth in order to tell you what you want to hear. As I explain in the ego discourses, what caused people to get stuck in the duality consciousness was that they lost contact with their spiritual teachers. The key to overcoming the duality consciousness is that you must establish a direct, personal contact with the Spirit of Truth, the Christ consciousness.

All outer teachings given by the ascended masters are given for the purpose of providing a bridge. If the students make the best possible use of the teaching, they can walk across the bridge and attain the Christ consciousness. The true purpose of a spiritual teacher is *not* to impart outer knowledge but to impart the teacher's consciousness to the student.

If students refuse to use the teaching or if they allow their egos to misuse the teaching, they will not reestablish the direct, inner connection to the ascended teachers. Their egos can even use an otherwise genuine teaching to keep the students separated from the teachers while being convinced that they are so advanced that they are guaranteed to be saved. This is self-righteousness, and I denounced it forcefully in the scribes and Pharisees.

In short, if you are a smart spiritual seeker, you will look for a teaching which challenges you to see what you cannot see on your own. If you are following a teaching which does not challenge you, it is time to look for another one that will challenge you. If you are not willing to let a spiritual teaching challenge you, you simply have not become fully teachable. I realize some people are not yet ready to let go of their most cherished illusions. A word to the wise should be sufficient.

3 | WHAT THE SOUL IS AND IS NOT

In the previous book, we talked about the soul, but we haven't really defined what it is. Some people wonder whether the soul is physical, spiritual or both? Can you give further teachings on how you want to define soul, lifestream, Conscious You and I AM Presence.

Over time, certain words can be used so widely that their meaning becomes watered down to the point where they are virtually useless. The word "soul" is used by almost all religious and spiritual teachings and they often use it differently. Rather than going into a detailed discussion about how different teachings use the word, let me give a concentrated teaching on how the ascended masters prefer to define these concepts at the present time. I am quite aware that we have used the word "soul" differently in the past, but here is how we prefer to use it today.

Let me begin with the I AM Presence. I have said that everything in the world of form is made from energy so the I AM Presence does have an energy component. It is obviously energy that vibrates at the much higher frequencies of the spiritual realm, meaning it is far above the energy spectrum that makes up the material world. The I AM Presence is more than energy because it is also Presence, meaning awareness or consciousness. This consciousness is what defines your unique individuality. Your I AM Presence is different from that of any other self-aware being.

Everything is made from a base energy, what we call the Ma-ter light, that can take on any form. However, this energy cannot take on form by itself. What causes the energy to take on a specific form is that a self-aware being formulates a mental image of the form and then projects it upon the Ma-ter light. The core of your I AM Presence is consciousness, but part of your Presence is what we call the causal body. This body is made partly from memories of your successful learning experiences and partly from the energy you qualified with a vibration of love. Over time, you build the volume and intensity of this causal body and by consciously connecting to it, you can express the fullness of your accumulated creative potential.

Because the I AM Presence contains only energies of a higher frequency than the material world, the Presence cannot be negatively affected by anything you encounter on earth. The I AM presence can never be destroyed, which also means that it cannot take embodiment. In order to take embodiment in a realm as dense as earth, the I AM Presence must create an extension of itself, which is what we today call the Conscious You. This self is pure awareness, meaning it really has no individuality built into it. This is a safety mechanism because it means that the Conscious You can descend into the material world but can never be destroyed by anything that happens in that realm. The Conscious You can never be lost.

The Conscious You derives its individuality from being an open door through which the I AM Presence can express itself. We can compare the Conscious You to a lens that works both ways. The Presence can express itself through the lens and can experience the material world—from the inside. However, the Conscious You does have free will and it is charged with making choices based on the perspective it has while in embodiment.

The Conscious You cannot interact directly with a physical body because the vibrations of matter are currently so low or dense on planet earth. The Conscious You must create a vehicle that can act as an intermediary between itself and the body. This vehicle has four components, namely the identity, mental, emotional and physical levels. We can call these four levels of the mind or even four lower bodies. It is the three higher "bodies" that make up the vehicle that most religious and spiritual teachings call the soul.

We of the ascended masters don't really have a problem with using the word "soul" in its broad sense, but there is an important dimension that is added by making the distinction between the Conscious You and the soul vehicle. Many spiritual teachings say that the soul was created in the spiritual realm and that it descends into physical bodies over many lifetimes. However, this teaching cannot fully explain why there are some souls that are prone to such tremendous evil while other souls are prone only to good.

This is explained when you understand that the Conscious You has created the soul over many lifetimes. It is the choices of the Conscious You that has defined the soul and determines whether it is prone towards evil or good. Hitler or Stalin were not created evil by God; they became evil as the result of choices made over many lifetimes.

This also adds the important distinction that it is not the goal of the spiritual path to perfect the soul. Instead, it is the goal of the Conscious You to actually give up the soul in order to ascend. You might notice that I said that only the man who descended from heaven can ascend back to heaven. I also told people to give up their lives (the life of the soul) in order to follow me, and while hanging on the cross I gave up the last "Ghost," meaning aspect of my soul vehicle.

This is important when you add the concept of the human ego. The ego is a part of the soul and it defines itself as a separate being. The ego will never be able to see itself as one with the I AM Presence. The Conscious You can see its oneness with the Presence, and this is the essence of Christhood (I and my Father are one). However, the Conscious You cannot do this as long as it perceives life through the perception filter of the ego and the soul. Many people have become so identified with the ego and the soul that they think this is where their individuality is anchored.

Even some spiritual seekers think they need to perfect this outer individuality and make it live up to a certain standard defined by a spiritual teaching. This is a fallacy that can take you into a blind alley for a very long time. Instead, the real path to Christhood is to return to the state of pure awareness with which the Conscious You first descended (unless you become as a little child, you cannot enter the kingdom) by gradually shedding elements of the ego and the soul.

I generally use the word "lifestream" to refer to the combination of the soul vehicle, the ego and the Conscious You. In some cases, I use it to refer to the totality of who you are, meaning it includes the I AM Presence. I have used the word "soul" when only talking about that which has become hurt, fragmented or can become lost. The Conscious You walks the path to Christhood by disidentifying itself from the soul vehicle and the ego. [NOTE: For more detailed teachings on this complex and important topic, see the book *The Power of Self.*]

What do you mean when you say that the soul can become lost?

As I define it here, the soul is a vehicle made by the Conscious You and it is made from energies that vibrate at the level of the material realm (at the identity, mental, emotional and physical levels). These energies originally came from the I AM Presence, and you grow by requalifying them so they can rise and become part of your causal body.

When I say that the Conscious You must surrender all aspects of the soul vehicle, I mean that it surrenders all attachments to the soul and all sense of being identified with it. I have also said that God has made you responsible for your use of energy and that all energy qualified with a lower vibration must be requalified by you before you are free to ascend. As you walk the path to Christhood, you raise the vibration of all lower energies in your soul vehicle, which means these energies now rise and add to the momentum of your causal body.

For people who are in a downward spiral, the situation is different. They will accumulate more and more lower energies in their soul vehicles. Because like attracts like, the immense amount of misqualified energies in the energy field around earth will exercise a magnetic pull on your personal energy field. This will cause energy to leak out slowly or if you experience a very traumatic situation, a fragment of your soul vehicle can actually be separated and "lost" in, for example, the emotional realm.

This fragmentation can eventually become so severe that the Conscious You loses its ability to retreive the soul fragments and energies and they are absorbed into the material realm. The Conscious You can give up on trying to retrieve them and retreat to the level of the I AM presence. The energies that could have been an addition to the creative momentum of your causal body are now lost.

What exactly is it that reincarnates? Which part of us is immortal and which is mortal?

It was the Conscious You that originally came from the spiritual realm, and only the Conscious You can ascend back to that realm. When the Conscious You has created the soul, then it will carry that vehicle with it from lifetime to lifetime so both the Conscious You and the soul reincarnate. The ego will likewise follow you from embodiment to embodiment.

In its pure form, the soul is a reflection of the individuality anchored in the I AM Presence, and we can talk about a pure soul. Such a soul will serve the Conscious You as a very good vehicle for acting as a co-creator through a physical body. The soul is still made from the energies of the material realm, and that is why it is simply given up as you go through the ascension process. As I said, the energies are requalified and become part of your "treasure laid up in heaven."

As I have already mentioned, the permanent part of your being is the I AM Presence. The Conscious You is the extension that the spiritual self creates in order to experience the material realm and serve as a co-creator with God. Although the Conscious You is an extension of the spiritual self, it is not created with the full awareness of the I AM Presence. It is indeed one of the purposes of the Conscious You to gradually acquire this God awareness through its journey in the material realm. When the Conscious You does acquire this awareness and realizes that it is an extension of the I AM Presence and an individualization of God, the Conscious You attains Christ consciousness. After that, the Conscious You can ascend to the spiritual realm and attain immortality by uniting with the

I AM Presence. The Conscious You literally merges back into the I AM Presence, but the Presence has become more because of the journey undertaken by the Conscious You.

You now become a member of the ascended masters, and we are all immortal beings. This is the potential that every Conscious You has, but the Conscious You must win its ascension by making the choices that lead to Christ consciousness, instead of making choices that will trap it in a lower sense of identity.

Because the Conscious You has free will, it has the potential to create its own sense of identity and its own sense of reality. This does not mean that the Conscious You can create a permanent reality that is outside of God. But it does mean that the Conscious You can create a sense of identity and reality that it believes is real and permanent, call it the ego or the soul. As long as the Conscious You clings to this imperfect sense of identity, and sees itself as separated from God or even in opposition to God, it cannot win its immortality.

The vast majority of people on this planet are not on the path to Christhood and are still identified with the ego created out of the illusion of separation. When I came to earth 2,000 years ago, it was to demonstrate that there is a viable path that leads to Christ consciousness and thereby to immortality— what I called eternal life (John 6:54). I came to set an example that all people could follow. Unfortunately, the very religion that claims to represent me on earth has turned me into an idol, put me on a pedestal and defined it as blasphemy if people claim they can follow in the footsteps of Jesus Christ.

This is a perfect example of the kind of false reality and identity that human beings can create. Obviously, it is erroneous, and I can assure you that Christianity in its present form is quite mortal and simply cannot survive in the long run. It will quickly begin to deteriorate in this new millennium, unless it goes through a spiritual resurrection and is realigned with my true teachings.

Some spiritual teachings say that our souls are still traumatized by the original birth when God gave us free will and that we still feel abandoned. Is that right?

Your soul is not traumatized from your original spiritual birth because that was the birth of your I AM Presence and then the birth of the Conscious You. That birth happened before your soul came into existence.

Your soul was created by your Conscious You as a vehicle for experiencing and acting in the material universe. Your soul was not traumatized when it was created because that was done based on some connection to the I AM Presence. It is entirely possible to create a pure soul and use that soul until the Conscious You has fulfilled its purpose for being in embodiment and then ascends. The soul does not have to ever become traumatized.

The trauma of the soul occurs when you descend into the death consciousness and become blinded by the illusion that you are a separate being. Because the Conscious You is pure awareness, it cannot be traumatized by anything in the material world, but the soul can be deeply affected by trauma. As long as the Conscious You identifies with the soul, it will experience life through the perception filter created by a traumatic experience. This is exactly what the dark forces want, and they want you to stay in that catch-22 indefinitely.

Your soul is traumatized from what some people call the original birth, but which was in reality the fall into a lower state of consciousness. This caused the Conscious You to see itself through the filter of the traumatized soul, meaning it now sees itself as separated from the I AM Presence. This event did cause many souls to feel abandoned, but the reality of the situation is that your Conscious You was not abandoned by God. Your Conscious You turned away from God and the I AM Presence, and because God respects your free will, he could do nothing to interfere with your choice. Once separated from God, it is possible that a Conscious You can believe that it did not exist before this separation. A traumatized soul might see the separation as its original birth. However, the separation from God was not the birth of the soul; it was the birth of the ego.

Some people say that when God created us as unique individuals, he set the stage for the many conflicts you see on earth.

God created you uniquely but there is no competition and no sense of conflict between your I AM Presence and the I AM Presence of any other lifestream. The clashes that occur between people are not clashes between their spiritual selves or even between their souls. They are clashes between their human egos.

The Conscious You does have a challenge that is inherent in its existence. It has to figure out how to maintain a sense of individuality while at the same time being part of a larger whole, including the I AM Presence and the entire Body of God—meaning other people. This is a challenge that the Conscious You usually takes a long time to resolve. This happens gradually as the Conscious You matures and defines its own sense of identity, partly as a result of the experiences it has in the material world. This challenge is not fully resolved until the Conscious You attains spiritual mastery, meaning Christ consciousness. It then sees itself as one with the I AM Presence and one with all life. God created your lifestream as a unique facet in a beautiful diamond. Each facet is unique but it is also part of the diamond. Each facet enhances the whole, yet the whole is more than the sum of its parts. The facet is complete only when it sees itself as being both unique and part of a larger whole. The differences between you and other lifestreams do not degrade or compete with your uniqueness. The fact that other lifestreams are different only enhances your uniqueness. As long as a Conscious You feels connected to its I AM Presence, it can see itself as part of a larger whole without feeling threatened by differences. When the Conscious You loses this connection, it no longer sees a connection between itself and other people, and that becomes the open door for the sense of competition and conflict.

God created your lifestream with unique characteristics because God wanted you to bring a gift to this universe that no other lifestream could possibly bring. You have the potential to be a co-creator with God here on earth and to bring a unique and uniquely precious gift to the forward movement of humankind. I admit that once the Conscious You perceives life through the filter of the death consciousness, individuality can pose a major challenge. It is the sense of separation that creates the challenge, and by walking the spiritual path and attaining personal Christhood, the Conscious You can reestablish its connection to the spiritual self. Thereby, you will begin to focus your attention on expressing your unique individuality and become less concerned about the actions and beliefs of other people. You will focus on being who you are, and you will let other people be who they are—or who they choose to be at the moment. You will be and let be, which is the key to peace of mind.

You mentioned that our souls can be wounded and that we need to heal our souls in order to complete the spiritual path. Is there such a thing as a disease of the soul? For example, is schizophrenia an illness of the soul, the mind or the body?

Diseases of the soul, such as Schizophrenia, is a complex topic because the medical profession does not have a very clear definition of most soul diseases. Schizophrenia is a good example because many different symptoms are attributed to this disease. When you take a look at the wide variety of symptoms, you will see that most human beings manifest one or more of these symptoms in a milder form.

The importance of this observation is that people who are diagnosed with schizophrenia are not somehow in a separate category from other people. The reality of the situation is that the vast majority of human beings have the seeds of schizophrenia within them. There are simply a few human beings in whom the symptoms become so severe that they cannot function normally or become diagnosed with the disease. There are many people who manage to live with some or all of the symptoms without ever being diagnosed or treated. In many societies some of the symptoms of schizophrenia are considered normal, even desirable, behavior.

If you take the bigger view and step back from the details of the different symptoms, if you look at the forest instead of the trees, you will see that the common denominator behind the multitude of symptoms is a boundary issue. People who have these symptoms have trouble determining the boundary between what is real and what is not real, between what is part of themselves and what is not part of themselves.

These people have trouble determining who they are, and their thoughts, feelings and actions are often affected by impulses from outside themselves. With diseases of any kind, there are always three components of the disease. The material universe is truly a reflection of the consciousness of material and nonmaterial beings. When you look at the symptoms, you can see that there is definitely a physical component of the disease. Many factors in the body can affect schizophrenia, such as brain chemistry, hormones or viruses. However, the major physical component of this disease is a disturbance in the electromagnetic functions of the brain. Science is only beginning to understand the true functions of the brain as an electromagnetic device. I predict that in coming decades this will be much better understood, and scientists will indeed develop ways to treat electromagnetic disturbances in the brain.

These physical components are not the cause of the disease, they simply magnify the symptoms. People who have such physical problems might indeed express the psychological symptoms to a more pronounced degree than the average human being, and that is why they are diagnosed with schizophrenia. In such cases, it can be valid to use physical means, such a drugs, to minimize the symptoms. However, this treatment of symptoms should never be mistaken for a cure.

Beyond the physical component is what one might call the psychological or soul component. This is what most psychologists see as the main cause of all psychological problems, and that is why they believe that such problems spring from hereditary and environmental factors. The reality is that there is indeed a mind which is attached to a particular physical body. That mind is greatly affected by the genetic makeup of the person's parents and the environmental factors that the person is exposed to during his or her upbringing. However, once again this outer mind is not the cause of the symptoms, it simply magnifies the symptoms. The soul is the ongoing aspect of your being. It survives the death of the physical body, and when the physical body dies, so does the body mind.

The only way for the Conscious You to express itself in the material world is through the filter of the outer mind and personality and the physical body. What happens is that the body and the outer mind will magnify conditions that are already found in the soul itself. One might even say that the outer mind and body are reflections of the conditions found in the soul. The lifestream is attracted to that particular body precisely because the conditions of the outer mind and body can help the lifestream resolve certain issues. If a lifestream comes into embodiment with a specific goal of overcoming a mental disease, such as schizophrenia, it will seek out a body and mind that will magnify the symptoms of this disease and help itself deal with them.

The real cause of schizophrenia is found in the soul. The good news is that any condition of the soul is treatable and curable. The bad news is that it takes work and that there are certain conditions that make it very difficult for the person to perform this work. One such condition is severe cases of schizophrenia. To understand this, let me give you a deeper understanding of the soul.

The soul vehicle is created as a complete unit with a crystalline structure. This means you have a clearly defined sense of identity with clearly defined boundaries. Before the Fall of Man, planet earth did not have any of the negative conditions found in the world today. Lifestreams could descend into the material world and take on a physical body without being exposed to some of the traumatic experiences that are common in today's world. This meant that the lifestream ran virtually no risk of having its original matrix and blueprint fragmented or destroyed.

After the Fall of Man, a number of imperfect conditions started appearing on this planet. This meant that many lifestreams were now exposed to traumatic experiences that were never part of God's original plan. The reality of the situation is that the Conscious You is an instrument for experiencing the material world and for helping to co-create this world. The Conscious You has a desire to experience the positive aspects of the material world, but it has no desire to experience the imperfect conditions that are currently found on this planet. When the Conscious You is in a physical body and is exposed to a very traumatic situation, the Conscious You can indeed decide that it does not want to experience that situation. However, because the Conscious You is trapped in the body, it cannot escape the situation. What happens in such situations is that the soul vehicle fragments; it splits into two or more smaller parts.

You might have heard the saying that nature abhors a vacuum. When a part of the soul vehicle has been split off, there is a vacuum inside the crystalline structure, and something is going to fill that vacuum. Because of the imperfect conditions found on this planet, it is highly likely that the vacuum is invaded by non-material beings. These can be malicious entities, such as demons. They can be discarnate lifestreams, whose bodies have died but the lifestreams have not moved on to the spiritual realm. It can also be parts of other lifestreams.

When a soul's crystalline structure is invaded by such outside influences, the Conscious You finds it difficult to draw the boundary between itself, meaning the original blueprint of its soul vehicle, and the outside world. The Conscious You can no longer discern what is of itself and what is an external influence; it can no longer discern what is real and what is unreal.

I can tell you that due to the violent past of planet earth, there are very few people who have complete and whole soul vehicles. The vast majority of human beings have some kind of split or fracture in their souls, and they have been invaded by outside influences. For most people this invasion has not reached a critical mass that prevents them from functioning at the level which is currently called normal, but which is actually far below the lifestream's true potential. [For profound teachings on the invasion by external spirits, see the book *Flowing With the River of Life*.]

For some people, the fracturing has become so severe that they do not have enough psychic substance left to have a clear sense of their identity. That is why their sense of identity begins to break down, and they experience difficulties in drawing proper boundaries around their identities. This can lead to schizophrenia, split personality syndrome and a number of other psychological symptoms. Most psychological symptoms known to man can be traced back to the fragmentation of the soul.

The only effective way to heal such symptoms is to help the lifestream regain its wholeness. There are many tools for doing this as already mentioned. In severe cases, such as schizophrenia, it is strongly advisable to seek the help of an experienced professional. I am aware that many schizophrenic patients will not be able to personally employ some of the spiritual tools I suggest. This is especially true for children. The parents of a schizophrenic child can employ the spiritual tools on behalf of the child. It is highly likely that the lifestreams of the parents volunteered to give birth to that child precisely because they have a great love for the lifestream and desire to help the lifestream overcome the condition and become whole.

Are there any spiritual techniques for recovering lost soul fragments?

There are a number of spiritual rituals and psychological techniques that can help the Conscious You retrieve and reintegrate soul fragments. I highly recommend that all sincere spiritual seekers study the topic of the fragmentation of the soul and employ various techniques for retrieving soul fragments. One of the most efficient rituals that you can practice on your own is the *East-West Invocation* given by Mother Mary. If you will follow her recommendation of giving one of the other invocations six days of the week and the *East-West Invocation* on the seventh day, you will indeed make tremendous progress in terms of retrieving soul fragments.

The misqualified energies that are stored in your energy field will fill up the vacuum left by a soul fragment so there is no room for the fragment to return. You need to remove these poisons, and this is partly a matter of choosing not to engage in negative feelings and partly a matter of transforming the toxic energy of the poisons. Mother Mary's invocations are designed to transform this energy, but so are the Violet Flame decrees we have given [See *www.transcendencetoolbox.com.*] Likewise, I highly recommend that people employ techniques for spiritual protection so they seal their energy fields from being invaded by misqualified energies. It is also important to protect yourself from non-material beings, such as entities or demons, by using the decrees and invocations to Archangel Michael.

Another essential part of reclaiming soul fragments is the love of your heart. As you grow on the path, your heart will form a magnet that will draw soul fragments back home. However, before your heart can become a magnet of love, you must have a certain level of wholeness. While your soul is still badly fragmented, your heart cannot hold enough love to draw soul fragments back. That is why you must start by clearing energies and protecting your energy field from the energies that prevent God's love from flowing through you. This is also why you need to invoke the assistance of spiritual beings, such as the beings invoked in the *East-West Invocation.*

As explained in *The Power of Self,* an important part of the healing process is that you need to make better decisions than you have made in the past and you need to replace imperfect decisions from the past. This requires you to go back and re-experience the decision that caused your soul to fragment. There are malicious forces who will seek to violently fragment your soul. These forces still cannot fragment your soul against your free will. They must trick you into making a decision that causes the fragmentation of your soul.

As I explained earlier, the Conscious You has two main functions. One is to experience the world of form, and the other is to help co-create the world of form. The dark forces seek to manipulate you into situations where you decide that you either do not want to experience that situation or you do not want to be a co-creator in that situation. This then is the key decision that causes the fragmentation of the soul. For example, when you experience a very traumatic situation, such as being in a war or being raped, your Conscious You might decide that it does not want to go through that experience, and this causes a part of your soul to split off while another part remains with the physical body.

The fragment that is split off now seeks to hide from the experience, and in so doing it often becomes stuck at a particular level of the world of form. To fully retrieve and reintegrate that fragment, you might need to go back and re-experience the original situation so that you can now decide that you do not need to fear experiencing the pain of the situation. You can go through the pain of the situation without fear, and in so doing you can free the soul fragment to return home. This is a process that can be greatly assisted through various forms of therapy that allow you to experience the painful situation in a safe environment and with the guidance of a qualified therapist.

Where exactly do soul fragments become stuck?

There are many places where soul fragments can become stuck. One of the most common places is the material world itself. For example, many houses are said to be haunted by former owners. The reason is that a substantial soul fragment of a former owner has become attached to that house. If the soul fragment is not large enough to maintain a separate sense of identity, it cannot evolve, and it remains attached to the house for a very long period of time.

Another common place for soul fragments to remain stuck is in what is often called the psychic or astral realm. This realm is a perversion of the emotional body of earth, and in this realm you find a large number of malicious spirits, such as demons. These spirits have literally created pockets in the astral realm that are very similar to the visions of hell that various people have had throughout the ages. If you have soul fragments stuck in one of these astral hells, it will behoove you to make a sincere effort to retrieve them.

Take note that because the astral realm is a perversion of the emotional body, the soul fragments stuck here are the result of highly emotional and traumatic situations. It is in such situations that the soul experiences fear and emotional pain and seeks to hide from the experience.

Do you recommend that everyone engages in therapy to retrieve lost soul fragments?

What I would recommend is that people apply calls to Archangel Michael for protection and Mother Mary's invocations for transformation and healing. On top of this, seek to sharpen your intuition, for example by using the technique for inner attunement that I give in *The Mystical Teachings of Jesus* and on the website. You will gradually gain an intuitive insight from your Christ self as to whether you need to do anything more to reclaim soul fragments. If you feel the inclination, by all means study various books on this topic. As you gain a clearer picture of the topic of the fragmentation of the soul, you might receive an impulse to engage in various forms of therapy. If so, by all means follow that impulse.

Because it is so individual which form of therapy will work best, I do not want to make a general recommendation. As I said earlier, when the student is ready, the teacher appears. When you are ready for a specific form of therapy for soul retrieval, your Christ self will tell you what you need to do. Simply remain open to inner direction.

Hardly anything compares to the healing power of having a substantial fragment returned to your soul. It can literally heal you instantly from problems you have suffered since childhood and often for many lifetimes. As I have said before, if the techniques that are available today had been in existence 2,000 years ago, I would have had all of my disciples engage in some form of therapy aimed at soul retrieval. Consequently, I would like my present disciples to also consider such therapy because it truly will open up for your wholeness and your service to me and to God. Because your lifestream is part of a larger whole, by healing yourself, you will help heal the whole. ✤

4 | THE OUTER AND THE INNER PATH

In the previous book we talked about a series of practical steps that people can take on the spiritual path. We started out by saying that in order to rise above feeling overwhelmed, people can use the two Rs, namely revelation and ritual. We also talked about a number of other steps that can lead to major progress on the path, and here are the main steps:

•   Increase your intuitive faculties and establish a connection to your Christ self.

*   •   Take command over your personal energy field by invoking spiritual protection and by transforming toxic energies stored in your field.

•   Come apart from the mass consciousness and the lies used by the powers of this world.

•   Reestablish the natural flow of unconditional love through your being.

- Use spiritual techniques to transform your karma from past lives before it manifests as negative events in this life.

- Heal your psyche of all scars from traumatic experiences, in this and previous lifetimes.

- Protect yourself from dark forces and rise above their influence.

- Learn how to use even the most difficult situations as stepping stones for growth.

- Overcome guilt, self-condemnation and the condemnation from the world.

- Heal your soul from all fragmentation and wounds.

I have to say that when I discovered the path in 1976, it would have been extremely helpful for me to have had the larger picture you have given us in the previous two books. I basically started walking blindly, and it took me years before I could begin to see the forest instead of constantly bumping into the trees. I also realize that at the time I needed something very practical, and I believe that such practical measures have helped me greatly.

I truly grew from applying various spiritual techniques, from studying outer teachings and from using various methods for healing my psychological wounds. I believe most people who are open to the spiritual path can benefit greatly from following these steps. I even believe that for many people this will be all they need for a while. Would you agree with that?

I do agree. Most people, who have grown up in a Western culture, were never taught about the spiritual path. They grew up with no clear understanding of the path and what it takes to successfully walk that path. The consequence is that when a person discovers the spiritual path that person is likely to look at the path through the filter of a set of beliefs and attitudes that the person has adopted as he or she was growing up. Because the Western culture is very practical and very result-oriented, it is inevitable that many people will have a practical approach to the path. They want a systematic process for attaining spiritual growth.

There is nothing inherently wrong with this approach. Hard work and constancy of effort is a necessary part of the spiritual path. You simply cannot attain true spiritual progress without being willing to make a systematic and determined effort, and, as I have said before, it will take time to break through on the spiritual path. I applaud the many people in the West who over the past decades have discovered the spiritual path – in one form or another – and have applied themselves to the path with great determination and constancy.

However, it is extremely important for people to realize that the spiritual path cannot be approached as most other activities in this world. The spiritual path is not simply a mechanical process, although it has certain mechanical aspects. Invoking spiritual protection, transforming toxic energies in your energy field and transmuting your karma, are quite mechanical tasks. If you apply a proper spiritual technique, you will gradually transform imperfect energies. Thereby, you will lessen the gravitational pull that drags you back into old habit patterns and thought patterns.

For many people it is necessary to go through a process of vigorously applying outer tools, studying outer teachings and following outer rules. One might say that most people on earth are trapped behind a wall of imperfect energy and beliefs. To escape this prison, it is necessary to use proper tools to gradually break down those walls so you can begin to look beyond your narrow mindset and reach for wider horizons. It is perfectly acceptable for many people to go through a period of focusing almost exclusively on the outer, mechanical aspects of the spiritual path. It is equally important for people to realize that this is only a phase, a certain cycle on the path, and there will come a point when it is time to move on and attain a greater understanding of what the path is all about.

If there is one thing I would like all people to understand about the spiritual path, it is that the path is an ongoing process. It will not stop as long as you are here on earth—for that matter it will not stop after you ascend to the spiritual realm. You should never allow yourself to stand still or to become stuck in a rigid mindset. One of the greatest dangers on the path is that people find an organization or philosophy that claims to have everything they need for salvation. If you believe this claim, there is a real danger that you will become stuck at a certain level of the path and thereby miss essential opportunities for further growth.

It is absolutely necessary that people realize the need to rise to the level where you begin to receive directions from inside yourself, namely from your Christ self and your spiritual teachers. Never allow any power on earth to get you to turn off or ignore this inner direction. If you will consciously strive to establish and maintain your intuitive connection, you can avoid becoming stuck. If you are a sincere spiritual seeker, you should never allow yourself to become stuck. No matter where you are – or think you are – on the path, you should always strive to take the next step. "From this point, forward!" is the battle cry of the most sincere and successful spiritual seekers.

This confirms my own experience. At the age of 18, I found an organization that promoted a simple meditation technique. It was claimed that by meditating 20 minutes morning and evening, all of our personal problems would automatically be resolved and we would attain cosmic consciousness after a few years. We could even solve all of the world's problems at the same time. Although this sounded very alluring at first, I soon realized that something was missing from the picture.

I later found an organization which has vast and profound teachings about the spiritual path and also a set of very effective techniques, such a decrees, for transforming toxic energy. Although I made great progress by using these tools, I eventually began to realize that the organization also seemed to focus too much on the outer application of decrees. There was a culture based on the belief that if only we applied the outer tools and followed certain rules, we would one day wake up and realize we had attained Christ consciousness. I gradually came to suspect that even though using outer tools can be very helpful, it cannot automatically take us all the way to Christ consciousness. Do you agree with this assessment?

I do, and for people who accept that the path is an ongoing process it should be easy to understand why. The key concept is the saying that when the student is ready, the teacher appears. One might also say that when a person first opens his or her mind that person will find a teacher, teaching or organization that matches the person's current level of spiritual maturity—or immaturity. There is a teacher for every level of consciousness. Some people have descended so far below the level of the Christ consciousness that they simply cannot recognize a true spiritual teacher. You will see from the scriptures that many people met me in person yet could not recognize my spiritual attainment. They saw me as an ordinary man or even as a madman.

It is important for people to understand that when you select a spiritual teaching, there are two factors involved. One is that you must recognize some truth in the teaching, and this recognition comes from your Christ self. The other is that you must feel comfortable with the teaching, and the need for comfortability comes from your ego and lower consciousness. If you have moved far below the level of Christ consciousness, you might be attracted to a teaching that tells you a little bit of truth and a lot of things that make your ego feel comfortable. The morsels of truth will help you grow—if you internalize them. The morsels of untruth can become a drag and prevent your growth—if your ego manages to make you accept them uncritically.

Most spiritual seekers will start their path by finding a teaching that is a mixture of truth and untruth. This is not necessarily a problem, as long as people recognize the need to never stand still and are willing to look for a higher teaching when they get inner direction to do so. The problem comes in when people allow their egos to make them believe that they have found the ultimate teacher, religion or organization and that it has everything they will ever need.

Such people often go through an initial period of rapid growth that can feel like a very dramatic improvement compared to their previous level of consciousness. After a while, the growth slows down, and the reason is often that they have advanced as much as they can with their present teacher. In order to grow further, they must transcend that teacher and look for the next teacher who is already there waiting in the wings but often not recognized by the person's outer consciousness. If people are not open to finding the next teacher, their egos will often succeed in making them feel comfortable where they are. They will then build a very rigid outer mindset with numerous sophisticated arguments for why they don't need to look beyond their present teacher. The teacher – who might have been a genuine teacher serving to take them to a higher level – has now become a trap that prevents their growth. Sincere seekers are always loyal to the path, to the inner teacher, instead of the outer teacher, doctrine or organization.

There are two main phases, or stages, of the spiritual path. As I said, for many people in the West it is necessary to go through a phase of being very practical and systematic about the path. You use outer tools to set yourself free from the gravitational pull of toxic energy, including personal energy and the mass consciousness. Doing so is following what we might call the outer path. The main focus of your attention is outer teachings, tools and rules. During this phase, many people can benefit from becoming members of a religious or spiritual organization that gives them an outer framework for walking the path. During this stage, the soul's attention is focused outside itself, and it believes that it needs something from outside itself in order to make spiritual progress, in order to be saved.

Billions of lifestreams on earth are today at the level of consciousness where they need such an outer path. During this phase, a lifestream is not yet mature enough to accept the fact that it has everything it needs inside itself. It needs the security of following an outer organization or teacher, which makes the promise that the soul can be saved by applying outer tools. That is indeed why you see millions of people who turn to a traditional religion or many of the new spiritual organizations that have emerged. Again, this is not necessarily a wrong approach, but it is important to realize that in order to complete the spiritual path and attain Christ consciousness, there will come a point where you simply must transcend this outer path.

This does not necessarily mean that you have to abandon an outer organization, a technique or a teaching. But it does mean that you need to rise to a level of awareness that allows you to see beyond the outer teaching. We might say that the outer path represents the beginning phase, the neophyte phase. When you reach the more mature phase, you need to step up and realize that the real goal of the spiritual path is to attain a new sense of identity as a spiritual being. You cannot rebuild your sense of identity by mechanically following the outer path. You can do so only by discovering the inner path that is hiding behind the outer teachings, the outer techniques and the outer rules. You can find the inner path only by looking within yourself, and the reason is that your sense of identity is the core of your being. You cannot change your sense of identity by using outer tools. You can change your sense of identity only by going within and making the choice to replace your limited beliefs about yourself with the truth about who you really are as a spiritual being. Rebuilding your sense of identity is not a mechanical process, but an artistic process based on choices you make.

Replacing your mortal sense of identity with a new spiritual sense of identity is a delicate process. Millions of people are ready to work on that process. Unfortunately, very few religious and spiritual organizations contain the spiritual teachings and the spiritual tools designed to help a lifestream discover and walk this inner path. That is indeed why I have decided to bring forth this and the other books. I am hoping to reach the millions of people who are currently ready for the inner path. I would like to dedicate the rest of this book to helping people discover the inner path to personal Christhood and help them anchor themselves firmly on that path. As a start, I would like to insert the discourse I gave some time ago that describes the different phases of a lifestream's growth.

5 | THE STAGES OF SPIRITUAL DEVELOPMENT

Jesus: When you survey the behavior, the attitudes and the beliefs of human beings on this planet, it should not be difficult to conclude that people are in many different states of consciousness, they are at different stages of spiritual development. These stages correspond to different degrees of understanding of the spiritual side of life. To give people some sense of comeasurement, I would like to give you a survey of the different stages of spiritual development found on this planet.

The following stages cannot simply be ranked from lowest to highest. A lifestream does not necessarily have to descend to a particular stage before it turns around and starts climbing its way back to God. There are many lifestreams on earth who never descended to the lowest stage of spiritual awareness.

Lifestreams who rebel against God

Certain lifestreams are in a state of consciousness that causes them to deliberately, and in most cases knowingly, rebel against the laws and the will of God. In some of these lifestreams, the rebellion is obvious. Some promote atheism or agnosticism. Some advocate scientific materialism and vehemently deny the need for a creative being. Some are openly practicing satanism, and although they do not deny the existence of God, they defame, belittle and ridicule everything related to God, religion or spirituality.

In some of these lifestreams the rebellion against God is hidden deep within the psyche, and it is often unrecognized by the person's conscious mind. This rebellion can often be camouflaged behind a facade of various beliefs, including religious beliefs. It might be surprising to many people, but some of the rebellious lifestreams have managed to attain high positions in various religious movements and churches. They claim to be highly religious and working for God's cause, yet they have a deep anger against God and believe they know better than God how the universe should be run or how people should be saved. These are the people that I referred to in the saying: "Beware of false prophets, which come to you in sheep's clothing, but inwardly they are ravening wolves" (Matthew 7:15).

For all of these people it is common that they are actively seeking to run away from God, to reinforce the impression that God does not exist or that he does not exist here on planet earth. Some of these lifestreams engage in an endless quest to prove that God does not exist or to prove that God is wrong and that they are right. They are literally seeking to prove that they can create a world in which God does not exist and in which they have no need for God.

You might ask how the people who work in religious movements can be said to work for this cause or to run away from God. The answer is that they use their power to cement the belief that God is somewhere "up there" in Heaven. These are also the people who cement the idolatrous belief that Jesus Christ is the only Son of God and that no one can follow my example. These are often the first people to cry blasphemy, as they did when I made certain remarks that made it sound like I was equating myself with God or calling myself a Son of God (John 10:33).

Lifestreams who try to hide from God

Many people are openly angry at God. Many lifestreams on earth have been hurt, and they believe that God has hurt them or treated them unfairly, unjustly or in a way that defies logical explanation. Many lifestreams are afraid of God and see him as an angry and judgmental being who is always ready to punish them for the slightest transgression of his laws. Common for these lifestreams is that they are running away from God but not because they are rebelling against God. They simply want to get as far away as possible from what they see as an angry, punishing and unjust deity. They are trying to hide from God.

Running away from God is an act of self-defense. These are the people that I referred to in the saying that I wish people were hot or cold (Revelation 3:15-16). The people at this stage are indeed cold. They are cold in the sense that they have come to accept a negative image of God, and they are running away from that image. However, they have the potential to turn around if they can come to accept that their feelings for God were caused by a false, imperfect or incomplete image of God.

Lifestreams who are indifferent toward God

At large number of lifestreams on planet earth have become so indifferent toward God, religion and the spiritual side of life that they have become lukewarm. Some of these lifestreams are indeed in a spiritual coma that makes it almost impossible to reach them with any kind of spiritual truth. Many of these lifestreams have been so hurt or disappointed by organized religion that they have rejected religion, or they have given up on the idea that they could ever partake of a true spiritual experience.

Many of these people have adopted a false, imperfect or incomplete image of God. Trying to help them see this and accept a correct image of God is very difficult because they often will not respond to any kind of spiritual message. Many of these people use the imperfections, real or perceived, of organized religion as an excuse for rejecting anything related to the spiritual side of life. If one approaches such people with a spiritual message, they will often become very suspicious and feel that one is out to convert them, to manipulate them, to take advantage of them or to get their money.

These lifestreams often reject all types of spirituality and thereby put themselves in a catch-22 in which they reject the very tools that could help them heal their wounds and get on the upward path. They are often unreachable for a spiritual teacher.

Lifestreams who are conflicted about God

Certain lifestreams have come to the realization that there is indeed some reality to the spiritual side of life and that there is a path they can follow toward a higher understanding of God and their relationship to God. These are lifestreams who have turned around and started the path that leads them back to God. However, many of these people have been so deeply hurt that they need spiritual and soul healing before they can earnestly engage in the spiritual path.

Some of these lifestreams have been hurt by physical trauma. Others have been hurt emotionally through their interactions with other people or the institutions of society.

Still others have been hurt by the imperfections of organized religion or have been scarred by so-called infallible doctrines that could not answer their questions about life. These wounds often cause such lifestreams to feel conflicts in their conception of or relationship to God. They might feel that religion doesn't make sense and presents a contradictory or inconsistent image of God—which is true for most mainstream religions. Or they might feel that a just and loving God shouldn't have allowed them to have been hurt. They often feel like victims of forces beyond their control and see no way to personally change their situation.

These lifestreams have come to the realization that they want more from life than what can be attained by material means. They sense there must be a place to go to find spiritual understanding and healing. They have been so deeply scarred and hurt that they are not yet able to start walking toward that understanding. They are like people who have broken a leg and need to heal the fracture before they can start walking toward their goal. Such people would do well to recognize their wounds and to focus all of their energy and attention on healing their psychological wounds and their souls.

Lifestreams who want to experience God's creation

A certain group of lifestreams are young lifestreams who have not yet spent a long time (meaning many embodiments) in the material world. Some of these lifestreams still have a great desire to experience everything in the material world, and this can make them indifferent toward the spiritual path. They are simply so preoccupied with the things of this world that they have no attention left over for spiritual pursuits.

Some young lifestreams are open to religion, yet they often approach it in a somewhat unbalanced manner. This can cause them to take their religious pursuits to the extremes. They often use religion not as a way to transcend the world but as a way to enrich their experience of this world. For example, they might seek to gain a position in a religious movement because it increases their status among men. These people have not yet had enough experience to achieve the balance of being wise as serpents and harmless as doves (Matthew 10:16).

Unfortunately, given the current conditions on this planet, it is common that young lifestreams, in their innocence, will be hurt or taken advantage of by both material and nonmaterial forces. This can often cause such lifestreams to lose their innocence and slide toward disappointment or anger. If such people are taken advantage of by organized religion, they might find it impossible to distinguish between God and the outer religion, and they become angry at God.

Lifestreams who seek to understand God

These lifestreams have consciously realized that there is more to life than the material realm. They know there is more to understand about life than what they were taught in school and Sunday school, and they have made the decision to start looking for it. These lifestreams have also healed at least some of their deepest wounds so that they have attention left over to focus on studying the spiritual side of life.

To achieve maximum growth, these people need to focus most of their attention on studying spiritual teachings, practicing various spiritual techniques and seeking to internalize spiritual truth and principles. These lifestreams can benefit greatly from following the outer path. These people are the "reason for being" of any true spiritual movement. It is their quest for understanding that gives the ascended masters great hope for the future of planet earth.

Lifestreams who seek to help others understand God

After a lifestream has spent a sufficient amount of time studying spiritual teachings and practicing techniques for spiritual growth, that lifestream has internalized a critical amount of spiritual knowledge. The next logical step is that the lifestream begins to give out that knowledge by teaching others.

One can be a student only for so long. When one has reached a certain level, the lifestream cannot learn any more until it begins teaching what it has internalized. Only by teaching others can the lifestream ascend to the next level of learning because it is through giving that you truly receive and it is through teaching that you truly learn.

The key to becoming a true teacher is to internalize the teaching, and in order to do that, you must discover and follow the inner path. People at this level need to discover the inner path instead of teaching the outer path. If they continue on the outer path, they will not reach their full potential, neither personally nor as teachers. There is a real danger that people at this level can become stuck or backslide into becoming representatives of the false teachers that seek to deceive lifestreams.

When these lifestreams follow the inner path, they are the backbone of any true spiritual movement. Without these lifestreams acting as our partners on earth, the ascended masters would have little hope for reaching other lifestreams with a spiritual message.

Lifestreams who seek union with God

As a lifestream climbs the spiritual path, it gradually becomes less attached to outer manifestations, such as a particular religion or spiritual teaching. It begins to see that there is a transcendent reality behind the many different expressions of spiritual teachings. It begins to see the universal path behind all of the outer religions, organizations, teachings, techniques and teachers.

During the previous two stages, a lifestream might follow one particular religion or philosophy and use it as its springboard for growth. This is quite acceptable, as long as the lifestream does not become stuck in thinking that its particular religion is the only true religion or the only valid road to understanding God. If a lifestream does become attached, it will remain stuck at a certain stage of spiritual growth until it begins to acknowledge the inner path.

When the lifestream does begin to see the inner path, it ascends to the level of becoming a mystic. It now realizes that the ultimate goal of the spiritual path is not to understand God but to know God, to experience God and to attain union with God. This is what I demonstrated in my life, and it is reflected most clearly in my statement: "I and my Father are one" (John 10:30).

Some mystics might withdraw from worldly activities and focus all of their attention on attaining the mystical union with God. However, in this day and age, many have the opportunity to choose to remain active in the world, and this is indeed highly needed. Such lifestreams can then demonstrate the inner path by example, and some of them can teach this path openly.

Lifestreams who have attained mastery

As lifestreams rise on the path and begin to teach spiritual truth, they will gradually begin to internalize more and more truth and more and more light. They will then gradually become what one might call masters in embodiment.

These are lifestreams who have understood some of the deeper mysteries, especially the difference between "doing" and "being." You will recall my statement: "I can of mine own self do nothing: as I hear, I judge: and my judgment is just; because I seek not mine own will, but the will of the Father which hath sent me" (John 5:30). When the lifestream attains mastery, it is no longer trying to do anything in this world. It is simply being who it is and allowing the I AM Presence, and possibly spiritual beings, to act through it. The lifestream has become the open door that no human can shut. The lifestream might serve to bring forth spiritual truths directly from a higher realm, thereby delivering the Living Word in its highest form. Or such lifestreams might serve in other capacities to advance and to demonstrate the cause of the ascended masters. These lifestreams can literally be our hands and feet on earth.

However, there is no exact standard for how a lifestream with spiritual mastery should act, or rather be. Some lifestreams might become world teachers. Some might live a seemingly ordinary life and can hardly be distinguished from the average person. Some might have severe handicaps or diseases. Some might sit in a cave in the Himalayas, or elsewhere, and meditate day and night to hold the spiritual balance for the earth. Others might even exhibit behavior that is not associated with spiritual mastery. A major goal for such lifestreams is to shatter people's mental boxes and challenge what they think is possible or allowed for a human being.

Do not misuse this teaching

Let me issue a word of warning. There is an inherent danger in giving any kind of teaching that allows people to compare themselves to others. Many people are still caught in the spirit of vain competition, and they will use my stages of spiritual development to judge themselves and their progress compared to others. They will then attempt to set themselves up on a

pedestal and judge themselves as being better or more important than others because they have reached a certain level of
development. Let me make it clear that as long as people are
caught in this state of consciousness, they have not reached
a high level of spiritual development. When you reach such
a level, there are no value judgments and there is no sense of
competition.

I am giving this teaching because it is valuable and important for a lifestream to realize its current level of spiritual development and thereby take appropriate measures to quickly rise
to a higher level. It is important for lifestreams at lower stages
of spiritual development to realize that there is a path that
leads them home to God. It is essential for such lifestreams to
discover that path and to anchor themselves firmly upon that
path. Likewise, it is essential for lifestreams at higher stages
to discover the universal, inner path to God. Such lifestreams
need to transcend their attachments to a particular outer religion and thereby realize the goal of manifesting their full
potential as sons and daughters of God.

Let me also say that the stages I have outlined here are not
meant to be seen as the only possible way to categorize spiritual development. One can take different criteria and come
up with other stages. One can also divide the stages I have
outlined and gain a more detailed picture. Indeed several of
the stages overlap, and a lifestream might be working on two
or three stages simultaneously. My purpose is to give a picture
that is not too complex and thereby causes people to focus on
details and lose the overall view.

When you do step back and look at the big picture, you
will see that the common denominator is that each stage represents a different way for the lifestream to relate to God.
The importance of this realization is that no matter where a
lifestream is in its spiritual development, that person is always

facing the challenge of working out its relationship to God. Every lifestream truly is a son or daughter of God, an individualization of God. The lifestream is meant to come to a full awareness and acceptance of its divine potential and thereby act as a co-creator with God in the material universe. The most important task for any lifestream is to resolve any imperfections in its conception of or relationship with God. That is truly what life in the material universe is all about. The goal of life is to resolve and heal all imperfections in the soul's attitude toward God. Such imperfections stand in the way of the soul's union with God and its acceptance of its potential to be a co-creator with God.

Why lifestreams descended to earth

I would like to give a brief teaching on the different categories of lifestreams that have descended to planet earth. When the earth was created, it expressed the purity and perfection of the seven Elohim, the seven spiritual beings who created this planet. In the beginning, most of the lifestreams that descended to planet earth fit into the category of young lifestreams. These lifestreams were innocent and had no negativity toward God. Some of them did have a great desire for the things that can be experienced in the material universe, and they focused most of their attention on enjoying this world. They had little thought left over for the spiritual side of life.

Other lifestreams were more spiritually inclined but had not yet firmly anchored themselves on the spiritual path and had not attained a permanent awareness of their spiritual identity and potential. Along with the young lifestreams were a group who had attained a degree of mastery. These lifestreams served as the spiritual teachers for younger lifestreams. For a very long time, the young lifestreams kept descending to planet earth without becoming trapped by the ego and the death consciousness. Many of these lifestreams did indeed ascend back to God after just one lifetime, although that lifetime was far longer than a normal life span today.

At some point, a shift started to occur on this planet. A number of lifestreams started becoming attached to or trapped in the consciousness of the material universe, and they started descending further and further into the death consciousness. One might say that these lifestreams started walking the path that leads them away from God, causing them to lose the awareness that they are spiritual beings.

As the consciousness of humankind was gradually lowered, it eventually reached a critical level. At this critical level it now became possible for certain rebellious lifestreams to start embodying on earth. These were lifestreams who had rebelled against God in a previous sphere or on other systems of worlds. These lifestreams are indeed rebellious, and for thousands of years a number of them have continued to embody on this planet. They have attempted to pull as many lifestreams as possible down to their level of consciousness and accept, even justify, their rebellion against God. These lifestreams are very aggressive and very ambitious in trying to prove their point that they can create a world in which God does not exist. They have literally influenced every aspect of life on this planet, including the field of religion.

The influence of these rebellious lifestreams has created a perilous condition on this planet. There are still young lifestreams who descend to this earth for the first time, yet there is a great risk that such lifestreams will be hurt by the conditions found on this planet. This can cause a lifestream to gradually slide down to the stage of being a wounded lifestream. It can then slide even further down and seek to hide from God, either because of anger or fear. It is even possible that the lifestream can descend to the stage of deliberately rebelling against God's will and God's law.

After the Fall, a number of lifestreams have embodied on this planet that are at higher stages of spiritual development, from being teachers to being masters. These lifestreams have descended on a rescue mission in an attempt to help other lifestreams find the true spiritual path, anchor themselves on that path and walk the path until they have regained their spiritual identity and can start the higher levels of the path that lead to the mystical union with God. Some of these more advanced lifestreams have indeed become hurt by the conditions on this planet and have descended into lower stages of consciousness. A few of them have even become rebellious against God because they could not maintain the connection to their higher selves.

Where are you headed?

I would also like to mention that there is a clear division in the stages. The center of the scale are the lifestreams who are young and who are simply experimenting with life on this planet. A lifestream is not meant to maintain this neutral stage for very long. Given the current conditions on this planet, most lifestreams will quickly be forced to go in one of two directions. One such direction is the lifestreams who have been trapped by doubt or have been hurt in various ways. These lifestreams now start moving away from God. The other direction is represented by the lifestreams who have realized that there is more to life than the material world. These lifestreams have discovered the path and are moving toward union with God. The two basic divisions you have on planet earth are lifestreams who are moving away from God and lifestreams who are moving toward union with God. The important consideration is whether a lifestream is moving away from God or moving toward God.

Lifestreams who are moving away from God are facing a perilous situation. Although there is a final limit to how far a lifestream can move away from God, there is indeed a very great distance that the lifestream can descend. The problem is that everything in the material universe is characterized by limitations. This means that the lifestream does not have an infinite amount of time to make it back to God. If the lifestream keeps moving away from God until its time is up, it will face the final judgment. If it does not respond positively, meaning that it is willing to take responsibility for its salvation and change course, it will be erased in the ritual known as the second death. It is indeed possible that souls can be lost. To avoid this scenario, a lifestream must come to a turning point. The lifestream must literally decide that it will stop running away from God and start the path that leads it back to God. It must come to the realization that: "I can't do this any longer!" What does it take for a lifestream to turn around? That depends on the lifestream's stage of development.

It is very difficult for a rebellious lifestream to turn around. Such lifestreams are often caught in spiritual pride, and some of them would rather die than admit that they are wrong. However, some lifestreams can eventually come to the realization that their attempts to create a world without God are futile. This can especially happen when they are confronted with a person who has attained Christhood and refuses to be changed by anything in this world. This did indeed happen to a few lifestreams who saw me during my embodiment 2,000 years ago. They realized that even though they could kill my physical body, they could not change my spirit, and this caused them to realize that God will eventually be victorious regardless of the appearances of this world.

A lifestream who is seeking to hide from God out of fear or anger finds it a bit easier to turn around because it does not have to prove that it is right. It is possible for such lifestreams to come to the realization that they have an incorrect or incomplete image of God. It was this image that caused them to be hurt, to become angry or to fear God.

Lifestreams who are indifferent toward God can be very difficult to reach for a spiritual teacher. However, these lifestreams have enrolled themselves in the School of Hard Knocks, and in many cases they can be turned around by a severe outer crisis. These people will procrastinate the acknowledgment of the spiritual side of life until an outer crisis forces them to realize that something is missing from their lives. Because they are constantly sending out imperfect energy, it is only a matter of time before the cosmic mirror reflects that energy back to them and precipitates a major crisis.

Lifestreams who are conflicted about God or have been deeply hurt can be turned around when they realize that God did not hurt them and God did not create the doctrines that gave them the conflicts about God. When these lifestreams realize what is truly happening on this planet as a result of the misuse of free will and the existence of dark forces, they can often go through an instantaneous turnaround in which they realize that God has never hurt them. Instead, they have been hurt by forces and people who rebel against God or who are angry at God. Such lifestreams will often realize that they have no desire to run away from God, and this will enable them to start the path that leads to their healing.

Once a lifestream has discovered the spiritual path and anchored itself on the path, it has already turned around. However, this does not mean that the lifestream is home free. The essential point for a lifestream who is moving toward God is that it realizes the absolute need to keep moving, to keep transcending its understanding of God. It is absolutely essential that the soul does not become attached to a particular outer expression of spiritual truth because such an attachment will cause the soul's growth to come to a halt.

If the lifestream does not see the need for constant self-transcendence, it can become stuck at a particular level of the path. If it remains stuck for a long time, it will inevitably start sliding backward. There are indeed many lifestreams on planet earth today who have discovered the spiritual path and who are walking the path. They have not yet come to the full realization that the path is ongoing. These lifestreams have not yet discovered the inner, universal path, and they have not yet become mystics. It is very important for these lifestream to recognize the ongoing nature of the path and the ultimate goal of union with God.

6 | THE SECOND TURNING POINT

You make it clear that the path is an inner path. Over the years, I have noticed that it is easy for people to believe that an outer organization or belief system is the key to growth and can give them everything they need. Some people are so preoccupied with an outer organization that they rarely direct their attention within. What is your response to that?

Once again, the key is to recognize that there are stages in a lifestream's growth. When a lifestream is lost in the death consciousness, it cannot clearly recognize a spiritual truth. When the lifestream is awakened to the spiritual path, it realizes that it needs a higher understanding, yet the lifestream subconsciously senses that it cannot get that understanding from within itself. That is why it reaches for an outer organization, doctrine or teacher. There is nothing wrong with this reaction. At the beginning stages of the path, a lifestream cannot get accurate directions from its Christ self because the Conscious You cannot see beyond the duality of the death consciousness. At this stage, the lifestream needs an outer guideline. The danger is that the lifestream can become attached to the outer organization, doctrine or teacher and refuse to go beyond it. What was meant to be an instrument for the person's liberation now becomes a prison for the lifestream.

I often see people who have grown up in a restrictive and closed-minded culture, such as mainstream Christianity, come across an idea or belief system which they feel contains a higher truth. These people's minds are suddenly opened to an understanding that is far beyond their old beliefs. In many cases, this leads to genuine growth. However, in some cases such a dramatic turnaround or conversion experience causes an unbalanced reaction. There are several unbalanced reactions:

• Some people go from the extreme of being too closed-minded to the other extreme of being too open-minded. They open their minds to any new idea that comes their way and become naive and gullible. As a result, they often do things they later regret.

• Some people think their new belief system can give them everything they need, and they close their minds to anything else. Such people have not anchored themselves on the true path. They have simply replaced one restrictive belief system with another one. This might lead to some progress, but it will not lead to continued progress.

• Some people not only throw away their old belief system but come to see it as somehow wrong, false or of the devil. They now engage in a crusade to prove their old belief system wrong. They fight a limited understanding instead of focusing their attention on getting a higher understanding.

Instead of these unbalanced reactions, I would like to see people open their minds in a balanced manner. I would like to see a constant, steady growth toward a higher understanding. For that to happen, people need to realize that the two most important characteristics of spiritual growth are constancy and balance. You need to be constant in your growth by seeing it as a process that will continue for the rest of your life.

Too many people have a conversion experience but instead of using that experience to anchor themselves firmly on the universal path of spiritual growth, they decide that the belief system which triggered the experience must contain the only truth there is. People had the conversion experience because they had opened their minds to a higher understanding. They now decide that they have found the only true belief system there is so they close their minds to any understanding beyond that belief system. No belief system on earth contains a complete understanding of God. To truly reach Christ consciousness, you must establish a connection to your Christ self so that you can get understanding directly from within. You cannot manifest Christhood by following outer belief systems. That is why the spiritual path is an inner path. It is an ongoing path that will continue for as long as you are here on earth.

The other aspect that I want people to embody is balance. The lifestream simply cannot exist in a vacuum, and I do not desire to see anyone throw away their existing belief system or suddenly become angry or feel that they were fooled or manipulated by that belief system. Whatever your current beliefs, you came to accept those beliefs for a reason. In most cases, the reason is that you needed to learn something from that experience. However imperfect your former beliefs might be, they nevertheless served as a teacher. They gave you a foundation for your personal growth, and if you use it correctly, the experience can be turned into a stepping stone for your progress.

Always strive to remain balanced. Open your mind to an understanding that is a little bit beyond your current beliefs. Once you have accepted and internalized that higher understanding, open your mind to an understanding that takes you a step higher on your path. I don't want people to attempt to take Heaven by force (Matthew 11:12). I want people to make steady progress so that the progress becomes internalized and gives them a firm foundation for ongoing growth.

There are too many people who fall into the trap of going from one extreme to the other. If Christians read this book, I don't want them to suddenly decide that their current church is completely wrong. I don't need people to start some kind of crusade to prove that their church is wrong or to convince other people that the church is wrong. I need people to anchor themselves firmly on the path and to keep taking one step at a time until they break through to a higher level of consciousness.

Too many people have a tendency to make decisions with their outer minds. Such decisions are always dualistic decisions. The key to spiritual growth is to overcome the relativity of the death consciousness. Contrary to what many people seem to think, the Christ mind is a very balanced mind. When you achieve Christ discernment, you achieve balance because you can see beyond the extremist and unbalanced beliefs that spring from the dualistic consciousness.

Unfortunately, some of the most closed-minded people are those who in their own eyes are the most religious or spiritual. You can find them in traditional religions and in many New Age organizations. Many religious people have used the outer doctrines of a particular religion to create a box around their minds that neither I nor any of my colleagues have the slightest chance of penetrating. It is a sad fact that millions of religious people firmly believe that because they belong to a particular religion and follow all of its outer rules and doctrines, they will automatically be saved. They also believe that their organization or teacher is the only key to saving the world so they direct all of their attention at converting the rest of the world to their belief system instead of promoting the universal path.

But almost every religion or spiritual organization claims that it has everything people need and that its members will automatically be saved. Are those claims wrong?

The idea of an automatic salvation is referred to in the saying: "There is a way which seemeth right unto a man, but the end thereof are the ways of death" (Proverbs 14:12). I often repeated that saying to my followers. I am Jesus Christ. I am a spiritual teacher. I know the reality of God and I know the reality of life on planet earth. I must tell you that there is no such thing as an automatic salvation. The brutal fact is that you will not be saved by wearing religion as an overcoat. You will not be saved by being a member of a particular church. You will not be saved by believing in a particular outer doctrine defined by some church authority. You will not be saved by practicing a particular ritual in a mechanical or rote manner.

You will not be saved by some savior, be it Jesus or Buddha or a New Age guru. You will not be saved by God, be it Allah, Jehovah, Brahma or whatever name you prefer. The simple fact is that you will not be saved by any force outside yourself. The brutal fact is that God will not save you. Then, how can you be saved? Human, save thyself!

✻ **I think a lot of people will find that a pretty tough pill to swallow. For the past 2,000 years, millions of Christians have come to see you as the Savior. Even many New Age people think they need a guru or an outer teaching in order to make their ascension. Now you are saying that you will not save people and neither will God or any other spiritual teacher so I think people will feel a bit lost.**

I have given you two pieces of information that explain the reality of the situation. I said that God gave every lifestream free will. I said that some lifestreams used that free will to descend into a state of consciousness in which they no longer have direct contact with the spiritual realm. This was not what God ideally wanted to see happen, but God had given lifestreams free will so God allowed it to happen.

People have a need for salvation because they have descended into the death consciousness. They descended into this state of consciousness by using their free will to make certain choices. The simple fact is that God cannot save a lifestream against its free will. If you are to be saved, you must make a completely free choice that you are willing to be saved. Salvation cannot happen in one miraculous event. Salvation is a process whereby you gradually free your mind from the dualistic illusions you have come to accept. You accepted those illusions by making choices, and the only way to overcome them is to make better choices. The essential element of spiritual growth is that you make the choice to leave behind one of your limited beliefs. The key to success on the path is that you never stop giving up your limited beliefs. You must be willing to do so indefinitely so that you never allow yourself to stand still or to become comfortable in a certain belief system or sense of identity.

It is absolutely essential that the more advanced spiritual seekers realize the sobering fact that no matter how high you have ascended on the spiritual path, no matter how sophisticated or advanced you think you are, there is always the risk that you can stop your spiritual progress. I earlier said that no matter how far a lifestream has descended below the Christ consciousness, the lifestream can experience a turnaround. The other side of the coin is that no matter how close the lifestream is to Christ consciousness, there is always a risk that the lifestream can decide to stand still and even go backward. The lifestream can, at any level of the path, decide that it is not willing to give up a limited belief whereby that belief now becomes the soul's God, its golden calf. The lifestream starts dancing around the golden calf – which it sees as absolute truth – instead of worshiping the true God, who is a God of continual growth and self-transcendence.

Unfortunately, this has happened to many people who have spent years or decades making great strides on the path. Some of them have finally attained important positions in an outer organization, and they can be reluctant to give up those positions. Others feel that after years of insecurity and turmoil, they have finally found a belief system and an environment that offers them stability, comfort and security. They are reluctant to give us this comfortable situation in order to grow further. I earlier said that when a lifestream first finds the path, it looks at the path through a filter. Remnants of such a filter stay with the lifestream until it attains Christ consciousness, and at any point of the path a lifestream can become attached to a certain view of the path and refuse to go beyond it.

The sad fact is that many mature seekers cling to the idea of an automatic salvation because they are not willing to take full and complete responsibility for their situation. I earlier said that before people can discover the spiritual path, they must be willing to take responsibility for their lives and they must be willing to change themselves. However, as you climb the path, you must expand your sense of responsibility and your willingness to change.

Let me give you an illustration of what is actually happening. A large number of lifestreams have descended into a state of consciousness in which they do not have a direct perception of or contact with the spiritual realm. These lifestreams are lost in the material world. How can a spiritual teacher help such lifestreams? You simply cannot solve a problem until you recognize the existence of the problem. We must begin by attempting to help people recognize the fact that they need to overcome their illusions. For most people this recognition comes through some kind of religion or spiritual teaching. For various reasons, this has led to the concept that people need an outer savior in order to be saved.

The problem is that when people lose contact with the spiritual side of life, they usually also lose all recognition of the basic fact of life, namely that they have been given free will and have the ability to create their own situation, their own "reality." People do not realize that the universe is a mirror so they do not understand how they got themselves into the outer situation and the state of consciousness in which they are currently trapped. They tend to feel victimized by some outer force and they either cannot or will not see that they have created their situation.

When such people first come to a conscious recognition that they need to be saved, they cannot accept the idea that they have created their current situation and that it is up to them to uncreate it. They need the idea that there is some kind of outer force that will do all the dirty work for them and bring them back home through a process that is beyond their control. Unfortunately, some people are reluctant to give up the belief in an outer savior, and even after being on the spiritual path for decades, they still think an outer organization, teaching or guru is the key to their salvation.

You are almost making it sound like the idea of a savior is an illusion. Is that what you are saying?

No, that is not what I am saying. Please try to understand that one of the characteristics of the death consciousness is that people tend to see everything in the relative, dualistic terms of black and white. If one statement is true, then the opposite statement must be false. People tend to think that everything must be put on a relative scale that is defined by two extremes, such as true and false, right and wrong, good and evil. They tend to think that any idea must fit on this scale and that the idea must be either true or false.

The truth and the reality of God cannot be forced into this relative view of the world. Truth is not relative, and it does not fit on a scale of what human beings have defined as being true or false. These are relative terms, defined according to people's current level of consciousness. You might say that the relative scale is defined by people's current mental boxes. The truth and the reality of God cannot be defined according to any of the relative scales or belief systems created by human beings. The consequence is that if you want to know the truth and the reality of God, you must make an effort to reach beyond the dualistic state of consciousness that causes people to define everything in relative terms.

When I make the statement that people need to save themselves, the relative human consciousness immediately causes people to say – as you just did – that the consequence must be that you don't need an outer savior. Since that contradicts the Christian doctrine that I am the Savior – or the New Age belief that you need a guru – it must be a false statement. People take a black-and-white perspective. The reality of the situation is that many people have descended into such a low state of consciousness that they have lost all connection with the spiritual realm. People cannot cross that gap on their own. Go back to what I said earlier about the different levels of vibration. The spiritual realm is made of vibrations of a certain frequency. In the spiritual realm you never find vibrations below a certain frequency. If you go below that frequency, you go into the material world.

When people lose contact with the spiritual realm, their consciousness becomes completely enveloped in – or attuned to – the energies of the material world. The energies of the material world are lower than the energies of the spiritual world. You cannot save yourself by using the energies of the material world. This is part of what is illustrated in the story of the Tower of Babel. People can attempt to use the energies of the material world to build a tower that will reach all the way into Heaven but they can never be successful. You cannot pull yourself up by your bootstraps. There is no mechanical or automatic road to salvation.

Once people have lost contact with the spiritual realm, they cannot regain that contact by using the energies of the material world. They can only reestablish the contact by using the energies from the spiritual world. However, when people have no contact with the spiritual realm, they cannot reach the spiritual realm and pull down spiritual energy. They do need an outer savior who can breach the gap between their current level of consciousness and the spiritual realm.

On a personal level, the savior is each person's Christ self, as I explain in greater detail in *The Mystical Teachings of Jesus*. However, because many people are unable to hear their Christ selves, God has also sent outer saviors in the form of spiritual teachers. It was my great privilege to serve as such an outer savior, which more than anything means a teacher or guide. God has sent many other saviors and continues to send spiritual teachers to earth. The real key to salvation is not the outer savior. God is ever ready and willing to give people all the help they need in order to be saved. God continues to send outer saviors who offer people the gift of salvation. It truly rains upon the just and the unjust (Matthew 5:45) because God is constantly letting the gift of salvation rain from Heaven.

However, on a personal level the key to salvation is not the offering of the gift. The key to salvation is the acceptance of the gift. I had the privilege of serving as an outer savior for humankind. I walked the earth and I freely offered the gift of salvation to everyone I met—and I met thousands upon thousands of people. I can tell you from direct personal experience that most of the people to whom I offered the gift of salvation rejected that gift. They either did not see what they were being offered, or they did not want to take advantage of the offering. The brutal reality of life on planet earth is that because God has given human beings free will, even God cannot save a human being. That is the meaning of the saying: "You can lead a man to water, but you cannot make him drink."

If a human being is to be saved, that person must make a number of decisions and gradually raise his or her state of consciousness. To be saved, your mind must be free from the illusions of the lower mind, the relative, dualistic state of consciousness. However, this is an ongoing process of letting go of your limited beliefs. It is not an instantaneous miracle whereby some outer force suddenly elevates you to the status of being saved.

One might say that the real gift of salvation is the spiritual path that gradually leads a lifestream to Christ consciousness. Following that path requires constant, ongoing effort. Many people look for an instant salvation and are not willing to make the constant effort.

You are saying that salvation is available to everyone if they will only accept it?

Yes. Go back to my image that every person's mind is surrounded by a box made up of current beliefs. How did people come to accept those beliefs? To accept a belief, you must make a decision. I admit that many people have grown up in circumstances in which they were programmed to accept certain beliefs. Nevertheless, no matter how much outer pressure you are exposed to, the fact remains that before you accept any belief, you must make a decision.

In many cases, people do not make conscious decisions, or they are not fully aware of what the decision entails. Nevertheless, an idea cannot enter your mind unless you make a decision to let it in. This is proven by the fact that, throughout history, so many people have refused to accept a higher understanding, such as that the earth is round and not flat. The only way to overcome a limited or erroneous belief is to make the decision to accept a higher belief, a higher understanding. The key to salvation is that you must continue to expand your understanding of life until you have fulfilled the requirement described by Paul: "Let this mind be in you, which was also in Christ Jesus" (Philippians 2:5).

What is the key to salvation? Is it that some heavenly being descends to earth and sweeps you up to Heaven? No, the true key to salvation is that you must put on the wedding garment without which you will not be admitted to the wedding feast (Matthew 22:2-14). The wedding feast represents the kingdom of Heaven. The wedding garment represents a state of consciousness, namely the Christ consciousness. When I said:

"Seek ye first the kingdom of God; and all else shall be added unto you" (Matthew 6:33), I was referring to this state of consciousness. To paraphrase my statement, I would say: "Seek ye first a higher understanding of life, seek ye first the Christ consciousness; and all else, meaning salvation, shall be added unto you."

Salvation is a gift that is given freely to all. However, until people accept the gift, they cannot begin the process that leads to salvation. That process is a path leading to a higher state of consciousness. People must expand their mental boxes until they see the shining reality of God.

To return to your question of an outer savior, people need an outer savior to offer them a cup of cold water in Christ's name (Matthew 10:42). That cup is a cup of spiritual energy and of understanding. The cup of salvation has already been offered to every human being on earth (at the inner level of the lifestream, of which the outer consciousness might not be aware). It is not a matter of whether salvation is available to everyone because it already is. The real question is whether people will accept the gift. Because people have been given free will by God, and because God has defined a law that no one in Heaven is allowed to violate the free will of a human being, people can only be saved if they are willing to be saved.

You mean the entire idea that there is an automatic salvation is false, even though so many religions claim that only followers of that religion will be saved and all others will be damned?

That is correct. The process of salvation involves two elements. One is the offering of the gift of salvation in the form of spiritual energy and understanding. This gift can only be offered directly from the spiritual realm. The consequence is that no human institution can gain a patent or monopoly on this gift. No human organization can turn salvation on and guarantee that all members of that organization will automatically be saved. Likewise, no human authority can turn salvation off and guarantee that nonmembers or nonbelievers will not be saved. There never has been and never will be any earthly organization or authority with the power to decide who will be saved and who will not be saved.

The other element required for salvation is, as I just explained, people's free will. You can only be saved if you accept the gift of salvation and follow the process of spiritual growth that leads to a higher state of consciousness.

I assume this can be used to resolve the old conflict among Christians concerning whether you are saved by grace or by works?

That is correct. Both are necessary. You cannot be saved without grace, but God's grace is constantly raining upon the just and the unjust (Matthew 5:45). In order to accept and internalize that grace, you have to be willing to raise your state of consciousness and that takes work. If you are not willing to do the work that is required in order to free yourself from your erroneous beliefs, you cannot accept and internalize the grace of God.

Are you saying that the works we need to do are not only outer actions but also the inner works of transforming our consciousness?

Exactly! Just read the scriptures and see how often I talked about purifying the heart or becoming as little children. Then look at how I rebuked the scribes, the Pharisees, the Sadducees, the temple priests and the lawyers. Look at how I rebuked those who did their alms, fasted or prayed in public. These people believed they were doing all the right things and that they were so good that God simply had to save them. They thought they could buy their way into Heaven, yet all of their outer actions simply were not the acceptable offering.

The acceptable offering is that you are willing to sacrifice the human ego, the death consciousness, the false sense of identity in order to win the true identity of a son or daughter of God. Consider the statement: "For whosoever will save his life shall lose it: and whosoever will lose his life for my sake shall find it (Matthew 16:25). What I am truly saying is that those who cling to their mortal, human sense of identity will lose their souls, but those who are willing to lose that false identity will find the eternal life that is only available through the Christ consciousness.

Are you saying that no single religion has every- 🕮 thing we need to win our salvation?

Correct. Imagine that you have a dark room with concrete walls. In the room are a number of people and as they fumble around in the dark, they discover some wooden blocks. Some of the blocks are round cylinders, some are cubes and others have different shapes. Some people ignore the blocks. Some people deny that they have any value. Some people start fighting over which block is best and they use their chosen block to hit other people over the head.

A few people realize that if you stack the blocks on top of each other, you can climb up higher. Some people keep climbing until they reach the ceiling of the room. They discover that it is made of a soft material that is impenetrable to light. When they poke a hole in the material, a bright light shines through the hole. As they see the light, they are instantly free from the darkness.

The analogy is that the dark room is the world and the concrete walls are built by human beings as a result of their misuse of God's energy. Human beings have sealed the room from the light of God. God has created the light that shines from Above and God has tossed the wooden blocks, representing spiritual truths, into the room. Because God gave people free will, God cannot force anyone to stack the blocks, climb up higher and poke holes in the ceiling. God can give people the means to salvation, but God cannot force people to make use of them.

If you are to be saved, you must realize that God cannot save you. If you are to be saved, you must work out that salvation through your own efforts. You must decide how much effort you will put into it and whether you will cling to one particular block or gather blocks from all corners of the room and stack them on top of each other until you reach the ceiling and poke a hole for the light of God to shine into your mind. You cannot turn on the light that saves you, but you can stop closing your mind to the light that shines upon all.

I assume the idea of accepting salvation can be related to the concept we talked about in the previous book, namely that we must remove the blocks to the flow of love?

A good observation. The key to salvation is divine love, and it is constantly flowing from Above. Your lifestream is designed to be a vehicle for God's love to flow into this world. That is why the key to your salvation is to accept the flow of God's love through you. Because you have descended into a dualistic state of consciousness, you have created numerous blocks in your psyche that prevent you from accepting God's love. Some of those blocks make you feel like you are unworthy of God's love. The key to opening up the flow of love is to systematically remove those blocks so that the natural flow can be reestablished.

One might say that the challenge is to be – here on earth – the spiritual being that you were created to be. You must stop denying your spiritual identity and stop covering it over by the artificial sense of identity that causes you to think you are a mortal, limited and unworthy human being. You must accept your true identity as a spiritual being, as a son or daughter of God.

People would do well to consider why there was such opposition to my personal mission. Why were some people so intent on killing me? The reason is that the last thing the forces of this world want is for you to accept your true identity. That is why they challenged me and accused me of blasphemy when I said I was the son of God (John 10:30-39). That is why they killed me when they could not silence me. That is why, when they could not stop the spread of my teachings, they perverted those teachings and created the idol that Jesus Christ is the only son of God, and therefore no one can follow in his footsteps.

But so many religions and cultures portray God as judgmental and his love as being given conditionally. I mean, we have been brought up to believe that unless we live up to certain outer requirements, we cannot possibly be worthy of God's love. Are you saying this mindset is not true?

Not only is it false, it is engineered by the forces who do not want you to accept your true identity. This mindset springs from duality and it is the primary reason so many people remain trapped by the death consciousness. God is completely and utterly above duality. If you think God's love is given according to any dualistic requirements that human beings could possibly dream up, you do not know God's love. You are worthy of God's love by the very fact that God gave you life. Nothing you could possibly do in this world could make you unworthy to receive God's love. Obviously, you are still responsible for any misuse of God's energy, but that is a separate issue from God's love.

God's love is given unconditionally to all lifestreams, yet what does it mean that God's love is unconditional? For one, it means that there are no conditions in this world that can make you unworthy to receive God's love. However, there are conditions that can make you *feel* you are unworthy to receive God's love, and they can prevent you from accepting what rains upon the just and the unjust.

Also, unconditional love is not blind love, meaning that it will not let you stand still in a limited sense of identity—it will not accept any conditions that prevent you from being who you are. God wants you to be all you were created to be, namely a co-creator. He does not want you to remain trapped in a dualistic sense of identity. Consider the following saying: "If ye endure chastening, God dealeth with you as with sons; for what son is he whom the father chasteneth not?" (Hebrews 12:7). The inner meaning is that God's unconditional love will not leave you alone; it will not leave you in a limited sense of identity. Because God loves you unconditionally, he will chase you like the Hound of Heaven that never lets you be completely comfortable in a dualistic frame of mind. You will always be on edge until you finally turn around, face your I AM Presence and allow the perfect love of God to cast out all your fears of letting go of the limited sense of identity you have created from the dualistic frame of mind. Consider the following statement: "There is no fear in love; but perfect love casteth out fear: because fear hath torment. He that feareth is not made perfect in love" (1John 4:18).

Being made perfect in love means that you accept God's love and you allow it to consume all unlike itself. You allow God's unconditional love to consume all the dualistic conditions that make you think you are anything less than the son or daughter of God you were created to be. Why do you think I said: "Be ye therefore perfect, even as your Father which is in Heaven is perfect" (Matthew 5:48)? You can be perfect only by letting unconditional love consume the conditions that make you see yourself as less than perfect. Consider the saying: "Every good gift and every perfect gift is from Above, and cometh down from the Father of lights, with whom is no variableness, neither shadow of turning" (James 1:17). There are no conditions in God, no variableness, neither shadow of turning, and you are separated from God only as long as you allow dualistic conditions to make you deny your true identity.

7 | RECOGNIZING FALSE TEACHERS

You make it so obvious that salvation is an inner process, yet so many religions have claimed that you are saved through the outer act of being a member of that church, and they have the power to decide who is saved and who is not. How do you explain this; where did this idea come from?

We could probably write an entire book explaining where this idea came from, but let me make it clear that it did not come from God. Organizations set themselves up as having the power to decide who is saved because human beings, or rather some lifestreams, have an insatiable desire for power. I think any person who takes an objective look at history should be able to see that there has always been a battle for power on this planet. We explain this in greater detail in *Healing Mother Earth*.

At any given time, certain lifestreams will attempt to set themselves up as an elite with a monopoly on power. These people want absolute power over the people. What better way to get such power than through an organization which claims that it has the power to decide whether you go to Heaven or burn forever in hell? If you believe an organization has the power to send you to hell unless you comply with its demands, you have given that organization the ultimate power over your soul.

I might mention here that the gift of free will comes with a certain accountability and responsibility. God has given you free will. You have the right to make completely free choices about what you believe. The consequence is that you have an obligation, a personal responsibility, to make sure that you do not give away your power to make free choices. It is your responsibility to make sure that you are making your own choices and not letting some earthly authority make choices for you.

God has given you the ability to make free choices. You cannot turn off that ability. Every moment of every day, you are making choices. Unfortunately, many people have descended to a state of consciousness in which they are afraid to make choices. As I said before, many people do not want to accept accountability for their situation and admit that their current situation is the result of choices they made in the past. Because of this unwillingness to accept personal accountability, many people have, often subconsciously, given away their power to make decisions. People do this by allowing some kind of earthly authority to tell them what they should believe about life.

The lifestream cannot exist in a vacuum. When the lifestream is trapped in duality, it loses the intuitive contact with its Christ self. The Christ self is the mediator between the Conscious You and the I AM Presence. If a lifestream has contact with the Christ self, it can always attain an intuitive understanding of a situation. When a lifestream has this understanding, it is easy for it to see what represents the highest possible choice. The lifestream can make choices that represent enlightened self-interest.

When the lifestream loses contact with the Christ self, it no longer has an absolute standard for evaluating its beliefs and actions. It has now sunk into a relative state of consciousness, and suddenly all of its choices produce undesirable consequences. Many lifestreams develop a fear of making choices. They fear that no matter what they do, it will lead to unpleasant consequences. They feel damned if they do and damned if they don't. This feeling is correct but only because the lifestream has lost contact with the Christ self.

As a result of this fear of making choices, many people want someone else to make decisions for them. They are looking for an outer authority who can tell them what to believe and how to live their lives. When you combine this with the fact that a small elite has an insatiable desire for power, you see the inevitable consequence.

The power elite will set up earthly institutions which tell people what to believe and how to live their lives. These institutions define outer doctrines that supposedly tell people what is right and wrong in an ultimate sense. They also define outer rules for how people should live their lives. In return, these organizations make the promise that if people will believe the doctrines and follow the rules, they will automatically be saved. Thereby, the leaders of these organizations become the false teachers that I spoke about in the following quote: "Let them alone: they be blind leaders of the blind. And if the blind lead the blind, both shall fall into the ditch" (Matthew 15:14).

I realize that most of the leaders of such organizations actually believe they have the power to promise an automatic salvation. They truly believe that they are working for a good cause and that their organization will lead people to the promised heaven. Most of the followers gladly believe the promise because it removes their personal accountability and frees them from what they see as the difficult task of making personal choices. This becomes an unholy alliance between those who want power and those who want to give away power. It becomes the way that seems right unto a human, but the end thereof are the ways of spiritual death—for both leaders and followers (Proverbs 14:12).

In my experience, many spiritual seekers are reluctant to acknowledge the existence of false teachers. I think part of the reason is that they cannot identify with the concept of false teachings promoted by orthodox Christianity, which basically says that anything that contradicts orthodox doctrines is of the devil. Could you comment on that?

A good observation. Let me again bring out the idea that the death consciousness is based on the relative, dualistic concepts of good and evil. When you are trapped in this state of consciousness, you tend to see everything in terms of black and white. You tend to think that everything can be defined in terms of two opposites, such as good and evil, and you tend to define good and evil based on outer criteria. One obvious example is the idea that your religion is the only true religion and that all other religions are false and will take people to hell. Finally, you tend to have a fear-based approach to life, meaning that you think it is necessary to avoid anything that doesn't fit your definition of good. This is what causes people to close their minds to anything beyond their religion, and it can develop into the fanaticism that makes people think it is justifiable to kill nonbelievers or those who threaten their religion. This form of extremism and lack of balance is the cause of most religious conflicts. As a lifestream rises on the spiritual path, it will reach a level of maturity that allows it to see through this black-and-white approach to religion. It will realize that fanaticism simply isn't right, and as a natural reaction, the lifestream will want to avoid all extremism and fanaticism. This has caused many people to reject the black-and-white viewpoints found in orthodox religious cultures. This is indeed what you see in many people who reject traditional religion and follow a more spiritual teaching, such as many New Age philosophies. As a result of this rejection of the inconsistencies and hypocrisy of traditional religion, people often reject many of the ideas promoted by traditional religion. This does indeed cause many spiritual seekers to reject the concept of evil or the idea that planet earth is a battleground between forces of evil and forces of good.

What I would like people to understand is that although this reaction is understandable, it is not the highest possible. The fanaticism found in many traditional religions is clearly an unbalanced state. One might say that it represents one extreme, namely a fear of evil. If you fear evil, you give dark forces power over you because one of the most effective ways to manipulate people is through fear. By entering a fear-based mindset, you actually make it easy for dark forces to manipulate you. You will attract what you fear.

However, ignoring, denying or explaining away the existence of evil is also an unbalanced reaction, and it simply goes into the opposite extreme. It can also stop your growth because you will not make a cancerous tumor go away by ignoring it. As I said earlier, when people are trapped in duality, they will define good and evil according to their own beliefs. Some Christians define people as sinners and say that everything you do in this world is sinful. This is one extreme, and it is based on a false definition of evil. Some New Age people define everything as good and say that nothing is evil or that evil is simply a necessary part of God's creation. This is the opposite extreme, and it is based on a false definition of good.

Both extremes are consequences of the death consciousness and its relativity and duality. Unfortunately, many sincere people, including many people who are truly religious and spiritual, have been caught in one of these extremes. They spend their entire lives defending a relative definition of good and evil, and they never reach beyond the dualistic state of consciousness to see the absolute truth of God.

The way out is to contemplate that there is something above and beyond the relative definitions of good and evil. There is something beyond the duality of the death consciousness. Until you reach a certain level of the path, you cannot understand this fact. When you begin to attain conscious contact with your Christ self, you will be able to see beyond the relativity of the death consciousness. It is essential for all spiritual seekers to realize that discernment is an integral part of spiritual growth. If you want maximum spiritual growth, you must sharpen your ability to discern what is an absolute truth and what is a man-made definition of truth—a relative "truth." This true discernment cannot come from following an outer religion or teaching. It can come only by going within and making contact with your Christ self and your spiritual teachers.

When God designed this universe, he defined a set of laws that ensure stable and harmonious growth. The key to this growth is balance, especially a balance between the expanding and contracting forces of God, as explained in *Healing Mother Earth*. The true definition of good or truth is something that is in harmony with God's laws and God's intent for a balanced and harmonious universe. Anything that opposes or destroys the harmonious and balanced growth of the universe can be defined as evil in an absolute sense. The reason evil exists is that God has created a number of self-conscious beings who have free will. As an inevitable part of free will, these beings have the ability to violate God's laws and go against God's creative intent. God allows lifestreams to do this because he has built a safety mechanism into the universe. As explained before, the second law of thermodynamics makes sure that if a lifestream is not transcending itself, it will eventually self-destruct. God is not really that concerned about someone making a mistake, as long as the lifestream is still growing. You might have made severe mistakes, but as long as you keep transcending yourself, you will eventually grow out of those mistakes.

A lifestream has the ability to refuse to transcend itself and its current beliefs. If this happens, the lifestream will fall further and further below the level of the Christ consciousness, and this is what has created a temporary force on planet earth, a force that opposes the balanced and harmonious growth of this planet. We might call members of this force "serpents," and they use a number of serpentine lies to ensnare people and prevent them from manifesting their Christhood.

I earlier said that if you adopt a fear-based mindset, you make it easy for dark forces to manipulate you. If you adopt the mindset that evil doesn't exist or that it is somehow necessary, you make it equally easy for such forces to control you. Unfortunately, many people in the New Age movement have accepted this lie, and it can severely slow down their growth toward Christhood. Some Christians feel holier than thou in their fear-based definition of good and evil. Some New Age people feel holier than thou in their rejection of evil. Both are equally unbalanced and therefore easy targets for the manipulation of the serpents. As you mature on the path, you need to rise above these unbalanced reactions and see beyond the dualistic definition of good and evil. You need to see that both the forces that are trying to break down everything and the forces that seek to maintain status quo work against God's law of constant growth. Only your Christ self can give you an absolute guiding rod for what is truly evil, meaning that it opposes God's law, and what is a man-made definition of evil.

The key to finding a correct response to the concept of good and evil is my saying: "Behold, I send you forth as sheep in the midst of wolves: be ye therefore wise as serpents, and harmless as doves" (Matthew 10:16). When you understand the inner meaning, you realize that you need to be aware that evil exists, and you need to be vigilant in terms of rising above the lies spread by evil forces. I earlier said that it is important for a spiritual seeker to realize that earth is a treacherous environment. One reason is that virtually every aspect of life on this planet has been influenced by the serpentine lies. There are numerous false ideas out there and there are numerous people and organizations who promote such false ideas, in many cases without realizing what they are doing. The key to rising above them is Christ discernment that allows you to see through the dualistic lies, combined with non-attachment that prevents you from responding with anything less than love. You are wise to the existence of serpents, yet harmless to their attempts to ensnare you.

How would you define a false teaching?

It is any idea which promotes a false concept concerning the reality of life, namely God's purpose for creation and the laws of God—including the fact that all people have a spiritual potential to put on the mind of Christ. We might say that a false teaching is any idea which prevents you from manifesting your Christhood. We can also say that it is any idea which seeks to bind you to a certain state of consciousness, a certain world view, instead of helping you constantly grow and transcend yourself until you manifest Christ consciousness.

I know that many people will want me to be more specific and say whether this or that religion or philosophy is true or false. However, as I have tried to explain, the picture is not black and white. The reality is that planet earth is currently so infiltrated by false ideas that there is no religious or spiritual philosophy that contains 100 percent truth. No philosophy has all truth, and it will be that way until humankind rises to a level of consciousness that prevents the serpents from embodying on earth. Likewise, there is no philosophy that contains 100 percent error. Everything is a mixture of true and false ideas, yet obviously some philosophies have a higher degree of truth than others.

Consider a lifestream who has descended far below the Christ consciousness. The lifestream experiences a turnaround and calls for a teacher. The person will find a teaching that appeals to his or her current level of consciousness. If you have descended far below the Christ consciousness, you simply cannot recognize absolute truth so you are likely to find a teaching that contains a fair amount of error. The teaching will also contain some truth, and if the lifestream internalizes that truth, it can rise to a higher level of consciousness. This will allow the lifestream to reach for the next teacher, namely a teaching that contains a higher degree of truth. If the lifestream continues to internalize truth and reach for a higher teaching, it will eventually make contact with its Christ self. It is not really a problem that a person is a member of an organization that has some error, as long as the lifestream is willing to look for a higher teaching. It is only when people become emotionally attached to an outer teaching, organization or teacher that they fail to connect to their Christ selves and abort their growth. The essence of the spiritual path is that you never stand still, that you continue to self-transcend. As long as you keep moving forward, you will make it to the Christ consciousness. As you become more mature, it can be extremely helpful to realize that there are numerous ideas that are deliberately designed to prevent you from reaching the Christ consciousness. By consciously recognizing this fact, you will make it much easier for yourself to avoid being ensnared by these ideas, just as it is much easier to avoid dangerous bacteria when you know they exist.

What is your definition of a false teacher?

This is a slightly more complex definition. In one sense, we might say that a false teacher is anyone who promotes a false idea, but this could easily become a black-and-white definition. We would need to add that promoting a false idea does not make you a false teacher on a permanent basis. Nevertheless, anyone can temporarily function as a false teacher by promoting a false idea, as described in the following situation:

> 31 And he began to teach them, that the Son of man must suffer many things, and be rejected of the elders, and of the chief priests, and scribes, and be killed, and after three days rise again.
> 32 And he spake that saying openly. And Peter took him, and began to rebuke him.
> 33 But when he had turned about and looked on his disciples, he rebuked Peter, saying, Get thee behind me, Satan: for thou savourest not the things that be of God, but the things that be of men. (Mark, Chapter 8)

This situation has often been misinterpreted by Christian preachers, but the true meaning is that, at that moment, Peter was serving as a false teacher by seeking to impose a dualistic idea upon my mission. As I have said before, the Living Christ cannot fit into the mental boxes created by human beings, yet Peter wanted me to fit into his box. Obviously, most people have certain false beliefs, and promoting them does not turn them into false teachers—as long as they are willing to let go of those false ideas when they are presented with a higher understanding.

When it comes to people, we always need to look at the person's intent. There are many people who promote false ideas, but they do so with pure intentions. They have come to see these false ideas as truth, and they promote them with a pure intent of helping other people. Such people cannot justly be defined as false teachers, although they are unwittingly working to promote the cause of the false teachers on this planet.

I realize that many Christians are so trapped in a fear-based mindset that they will disagree with this. They will say that anyone promoting a false teaching – according to their definition – is of the devil and will go to hell. It is a fact that we of the ascended masters are always looking for people on earth who can take part in our efforts to help humankind grow spiritually. We are always looking for those who can serve as world teachers, and we do not require such teachers to be perfect according to a black-and-white human standard. What we are looking for is the purity of intention, the willingness to change and the drive to self-transcend. As long as a person is willing to self-transcend and continues to do so, we have great compassion and understanding, even if the person still has some false beliefs. There are many examples of people who have been fighting for a cause or promoting a teaching that was not the highest possible. Because of their commitment to growth, they still made great personal progress and they inspired others to follow the path of growth. We are looking for an inner quality, rather than outer perfection. In that respect, it should be noted that all people need to continually expand their understanding of life. If you are promoting spiritual ideas, you should be willing to self-transcend and reach for a higher understanding. As you do so, you will gradually abandon false ideas and accept higher ideas. If you are not willing to self-transcend, or if you are not willing to look beyond a certain belief system, then you can actually function as a false teacher even if you have a pure intent. For example, many well-meaning Christians continue to promote orthodox doctrines with the best of intentions. Because they are not willing to look beyond those doctrines, they are actually serving the cause of the false teachers that seek to prevent humankind from reaching Christhood.

Finally, let us look at people who deliberately and knowingly promote false ideas. These are the lifestreams who clearly function as false teachers. The problem is that many of these lifestreams are extremely good at camouflaging their intent. They often portray themselves as genuine spiritual teachers, and they can gather a substantial following. In the end, they are preventing their followers from reaching Christhood and becoming spiritually independent. Many of these false teachers are making their followers codependent upon them whereby the teacher can steal the spiritual light of the students. The students literally become like cattle that are milked for their spiritual light by the false teacher.

Many of these false teachers have attained high positions in traditional religions. Many of them have set themselves up as self-styled gurus in the empowerment, self-help or New Age fields. These are the people I was talking about when I warned about the false prophets who appear in sheep's clothing but are inwardly as ravening wolves (Matthew 7:15) or as whited sepulchres filled with dead men's bones (Matthew 23:27). The best way to expose such a teacher is to consider whether the teacher is seeking to make you codependent upon him or her. A true spiritual teacher will always seek to help you attain Christ consciousness so that you become completely independent of the teacher and can get everything you need from a source inside yourself. A false teacher might entice you with many true teachings, but in the end the teacher will not allow you to rise above a certain level and become truly independent.

8 | MOVING ON FROM A FALSE TEACHER

I think the topic of false teachers is very important. On a regular basis I talk to or get e-mails from people who have realized they have followed a spiritual or religious teacher they now consider false. Some have come to this conclusion on their own, some have read something elsewhere and some have read what you say on the website. Some of these people are quite concerned about how this might influence their spiritual path, even into the future. I wonder if you would like to comment on this topic, since it seems to be a stumbling block for many people who sincerely pursue spiritual growth.

Let me first say that there is no reason for a sincere spiritual seeker to feel bad about having followed a false teacher or teaching. As I just said, every aspect of life on this planet has been affected by the duality consciousness. There is hardly a single person on this planet who has not been exposed to false ideas. It is virtually impossible to grow up anywhere without being "brainwashed" with ideas that spring from the death consciousness. Most people have been exposed to such ideas in a more organized form, either as an orthodox religion, scientific materialism or simply the general world view that people have in their family or society.

There is no practical way to embody on earth without being exposed to false teachings. As a spiritual seeker, you should simply accept the fact that you have been exposed to false ideas since childhood and that a major part of the spiritual path is to purify your mind of the false beliefs that have been programmed into it.

I understand that many seekers feel bad because they have now identified a particular teaching or guru as being false, and they realize they have been fooled. Let me ask you this: "What is best? To realize you have been fooled or to still be fooled?" Obviously, once you realize you have been fooled, you are no longer fooled. You have demonstrated that you have some degree of Christ discernment so why feel regret? What you need to do is to prevent your ego from getting you to shut down or divert your quest for truth. Instead, you need to build on your accomplishment and continue to sharpen your Christ discernment—which is the only and ultimate defense against false teachers.

You need to avoid the typical ego reaction that springs from black-and-white thinking, namely that you decide you will never again follow a spiritual teacher. The mature reaction is that you will never follow a spiritual teacher the way you did the last time. But the reason is that you learned from what you did the last time. If you had not done it, how could you have learned?

Do you get my underlying point? Life is a process of building your personal Christhood. This involves increasing your ability to discern between what comes from the One Truth of the Christ mind and what comes from the innumerable dualistic "truths" of the death consciousness. Currently, life on this planet is heavily affected by the mind of anti-christ. It is inevitable that you grow up being affected by false teachers and teachings. This is currently part of life on this planet so there is no reason to complain about it, although it is important not to affirm it as a permanent or unavoidable condition. Instead, a spiritual seeker should accept that part of walking the spiritual path is to learn how to see through and free yourself from false teachers.

This is not just for the sake of your own growth, but also so that you can demonstrate for others how to overcome a false teaching and still move on toward personal Christhood. Most of today's spiritual seekers volunteered to be the forerunners and demonstrate how to move into the consciousness of the golden age. Stop feeling bad about having been exposed to false teachers. It is part of what you volunteered to do so get on with it and make the best of whatever situation you have encountered. You are here to demonstrate how to overcome so get on with overcoming! Physician, heal thyself—and then move on to healing others!

Defining false ideas

Let me go beyond what I have already said about how to define false teachings, and let us begin at the level of a single idea. Many religious people are caught in black-and-white thinking, and they would define a false idea this way: Our religion is the only true one, thus any idea that is different from, contradicts or goes beyond the official doctrines of our church is a false idea and the work of the devil. This is not a very useful definition.

Those who are colored by gray thinking (meaning nothing is good or bad) might think there are no false ideas and that any idea is as valid as any other idea. Or they might define a false idea as follows: The true, universal teachings all stress the need to be loving and kind so any idea that does not affirm that this is all we need to do is a false idea. Again, this is not a very useful definition so we need to take a different approach.

There are many people who would love for this planet to be a very neat and tidy place where it is easy to divide things into good and bad. The reality is that because of the influence of the death consciousness, everything is rather murky. The most dangerous consequence of the duality consciousness is that it creates a veil – what the Buddha called Maya – and the effect is that it becomes difficult for people to discern what is true and false in an absolute sense. This also makes it difficult to discern between true and false ideas.

For example, many people would like to believe that if a statement is made by a true spiritual teacher, then it will be absolutely, universally true and it will be true for all time. Many Christians would like to believe that every statement I made 2,000 years ago lives up to these demands. This desire is, of course, created by the ego and its attempt to define an automatic path to salvation. The ego is attempting to make you believe that because you now belong to a particular religion, you no longer need to exercise your Christ discernment but should unquestionably accept the outer doctrines of your church. You can *never* let down your guard and your responsibility to discern from within. Let me give an example. I once made the remark:

> 3 The Pharisees also came unto him, tempting him,
> and saying unto him, Is it lawful for a man to put
> away his wife for every cause?

6 Wherefore they are no more twain, but one flesh.
What therefore God hath joined together, let not man
put asunder. (Matthew, Chapter 19)

Many Christians, including the Catholic church, interpret
this to mean that I said divorce is universally wrong. In reality,
this teaching was given to address a specific situation, namely
that many men at the time viewed women as a piece of prop-
erty meant to bear children, keep house and be available for
sexual pleasure. When their wives became old and were no
longer attractive, many men simply abandoned them and took
younger wives. At the same time, women had no way to make
a living so this was extremely inhumane and also created a
major social problem. In today's age, one cannot interpret this
remark to mean that divorce is universally wrong because other
considerations now come into play. Take another example:

Jesus saith unto him, I am the way, the truth, and
the life: no man cometh unto the Father, but by me.
(John 14:16)

This remark is true, but only when one understands that
I was speaking as a representative of the universal Christ consciousness. It is this universal state of consciousness that is the
open door to the kingdom of God and not a historical person.
People can access this universal mind directly in a way that is
not dependent upon an external savior or an external church.
Although the remark is true, it has been misused by countless
Christians to justify all kinds of abuse, from the crusades to
discriminating against one's non-Christian neighbors.

It is not quite that simple to label an idea as false. What is
true in one context and time period can be false in another.
What is a true remark can still be misinterpreted and misused

by the death consciousness. The old, black-and-white belief that an idea is either true or false is not useful for a mature spiritual seeker. You need to deepen your ability to discern.

The true goal of spiritual growth is to rise above the death consciousness and be reborn into the Christ consciousness. The goal of a true spiritual teacher is *not* to give forth some absolute truth – for any idea expressed in words has entered the realm of duality – but to help a specific group of people rise above specific dualistic illusions. The teachings given by the Buddha are as true as my teachings, but they were given to different people in a different culture and they address slightly different aspects of the duality consciousness. A more useful measure for evaluating an idea is to look at its intent. Is the idea given with the intent to set you free from some aspect of the duality consciousness?

A true idea is given to set you free whereas a false idea is designed to trap you in the duality consciousness. I realize this will be disappointing to some people, for they are still looking for the black-and-white way to label a false idea. There is only one way to escape false teachers, and that is to sharpen your discernment, which is a creative, not a mechanical, process.

The human ego cannot see the Spirit of Truth but is always seeking to take a statement from this world and elevate it to the status of infallibility. The only real way to discern between true and false teachings is to base your discernment on a direct, inner experience of the Spirit of Truth. The Spirit of Truth is beyond specific words, as words can be interpreted in different ways by the duality consciousness.

There is only one Spirit of Truth, and once you experience it, you will know that it vibrates above a certain frequency level. You can – in your heart, not your head – compare the vibration of any idea to the vibration of the Spirit of Truth. If your mind is pure and your intention loving, you will know whether any idea springs from the Christ mind or the mind of anti-christ.

As you sharpen this ability to read the vibration of an idea – which includes the intent behind it – you will have the ultimate measure for exposing a false idea. Most spiritual seekers – especially those who have already seen through a false teaching – have already started developing this ability. They simply need to continue without letting their egos, their emotions or their intellectual minds interfere with the process. Practice does make perfect so if you don't keep practicing, you will stagnate. In short, a false idea is an idea that is designed to trap you in the duality consciousness and prevent you from transcending the ego.

Defining a false teaching

Let us now take this beyond a single idea and look at how to evaluate a spiritual teaching, meaning a body of ideas assembled into a whole. The black-and-white approach would say that a true teaching contains no false ideas whereas a teaching that contains one false idea is a false teaching. If you apply this criteria, you will not find a single true teaching on this planet. For example, many Christians believe the Bible is a true teaching, but that is because they intentionally blind themselves to the errors and contradictions in the Bible.

Bringing forth spiritual teachings on earth and translating them into human language is a difficult process. Words are inherently ambiguous so even if you word a statement as precisely as you can, people can still come up with different interpretations. What seems true to one person can seem false to another. In reality, what seems true or false is not the actual statement but the individual interpretation of it. Against this, no spiritual teacher can protect his statements.

You also need to realize that even the best teachings will contain some errors in them because things are "lost in translation." Furthermore, you must consider the context in which the teaching was given. The ego wants to elevate a teaching to the status of being infallible, meaning that it is absolutely true in all circumstances and for all time. This is an impossible dream, for no teaching can be understood without being seen in context. For example, a teaching that is given in the East will be adapted to the mindset, culture and even the use of words in the area. If you evaluate the teaching with a western mindset, culture and use of words, you might impose errors upon the teaching that are not there in the original form.

On the other hand, it must be made clear that even a false teaching will contain many true ideas. If it had no truth in it, it would attract very few people. The more sophisticated false teachings contain mostly ideas that – seen in isolation – are true.

When they are seen in context, they are given a slight turn that can take the unaware seeker into a blind alley. This has caused many sincere seekers to follow false teachers because they focus their attention on the many true statements made by such a teacher. The teacher is saying so many things that they want to hear that they unconsciously – or sometimes even willingly – overlook the few warning signs that exposes the false intent behind the teaching.

Again, a better measure for the value of a teaching is the intent behind it. A true teaching is designed to help you rise above the duality consciousness whereas a false teaching is designed to keep you trapped while thinking you are a very spiritual person who is doing everything right. This can be detected when you use your intuitive faculties to read the vibration of a teaching.

Defining a false teacher

One of the most common mistakes made by religious and spiritual people is that they expect a spiritual teacher to be the perfect human being. They judge this based on the standard of their religion, society or even a personal standard. The trouble is that such standards are often heavily influenced by the ego, and the result is that no one could possibly live up to them.

Another important point is that a spiritual teacher is not meant to live up to a human standard of perfection. On the contrary, the role of a true spiritual teacher is to shake people out of their rigid mindset. A true teacher often appears in disguise or plays a role that challenges people's pre-conceived opinions. For example, many people rejected me 2,000 years ago because I did not live up to their expectations about how the Messiah – a perfect human being in their minds – should appear and behave.

If you look at appearance and behavior, you cannot correctly distinguish between true and false teachers. Many true teachers deliberately take on an appearance designed to filter out those who are not serious students, those who are not willing to look behind appearances. Many false teachers attempt to take on the appearance of being perfect according to the expectations of their target audience. A true teacher will tell you what you need to hear whereas a false teacher will tell you what you want to hear.

Again, you must go beyond the outer mind and use your intuition to read the intent and vibration of a teacher. Fortunately, this is much easier to do for a living person than for a teaching expressed in words. When you see a person, even a photograph, you can read the totality of the person's energy field—even if you don't see it.

In a teaching expressed in words, it is easy to camouflage or hide errors. No person can completely control his or her energy field, and a perceptive student can read the energy field of a prospective teacher. Many students have had an instant recognition upon meeting a teacher whereas others have been instantly repelled. However, this process is not always infallible, as we will discuss later.

Growing teachers and false teachers

Let us take this into a little more detail. As I seek to explain in these books, Christhood that is not expressed is not Christhood. The Alpha aspect of Christhood is that you establish an inner connection to your higher being, a connection that does not depend on and cannot be disturbed by anything on earth. The Omega aspect is that you use that connection to selflessly raise other parts of life. Only when you have this complete circle, this figure-eight flow, have you attained a degree of Christhood. For the most mature seekers on this planet, teaching others (or helping them in other ways) is a natural and inescapable part of the spiritual path.

If you take a brief look at the internet, you will see that there are many, many people who claim to be spiritual teachers, channelers or messengers in some capacity. Can we reasonably say that most of these are false teachers? That depends on what criteria you use. Teaching is a natural part of Christhood, yet you do not have to be perfect before you start this teaching mission. People trapped in the black-and-white approach will say that only a perfect person can be a true teacher. People trapped in a grey approach will say anyone can be a true teacher. The truth is, of course, beyond both extremes.

The fact of the matter is that there are many people in today's world who are seeking to teach others, yet they themselves are not perfect and have not attained the fullness of Christhood. Let me make it clear that there is not necessarily anything wrong with this. It is in teaching that you truly learn so if you do not start teaching, your learning cannot progress beyond a certain level. You need to start teaching before you are perfect. The big question becomes whether you will recognize and admit that you are not perfect or whether you will seek to hide your inexperience behind a veil of infallibility?

There is nothing wrong with a mature spiritual seeker trying to teach others. However, it is extremely important to remain humble and *not* let the ego talk one into beginning to play the game of superiority or infallibility. As long as you keep firmly in mind that you don't know everything and that you are constantly learning and growing, then you can still help others and experience personal growth.

Do you see the distinction here? Many of the people who teach do not have the highest possible understanding of reality or of the teachings of the ascended masters. They may even still have some personality flaws or unresolved psychological issues. They still have certain erroneous or incomplete beliefs, meaning that they might be teaching some ideas that are false. If their intent is pure, if they don't claim infallibility and if they are constantly trying to grow, then they are *not* false teachers. They may be immature, inexperienced or flawed teachers, but they are not false teachers because they are not deliberately and maliciously trying to mislead and manipulate others. If such a person is honest and sincere with his or her followers, it is possible that a group of people can make tremendous progress by growing together.

Those who have impure intentions

This then leads us to identify a group of teachers that we can safely label as false. These are the ones who are deliberately – and in most cases they know this consciously – trying to deceive others. They do this for various reasons, ranging from money over the need to feel superior to the need to vampirize spiritual energy from those who still have it. These teachers can often be difficult for inexperienced seekers to expose because they are very good at hiding their true intent behind a facade of sincerity, credibility, selflessness and humility. They are good at playing the game and giving people what they are looking for in a spiritual teacher.

How do you recognize such false teachers? Here are some outer points that can give you a foundation, but do not forget that the most important points are intent and vibration:

- False teachers are often very concerned about establishing authority for themselves. The purpose is to set themselves up so they cannot be questioned or gainsaid. For example, some Christian churches and even New Age organizations claim to be the only true representatives of Christ based on a lineage of people going all the way back to me 2,000 years ago. In reality, such an earthly lineage is worthless because it could so easily be polluted. The only thing that really matters is that you have the spiritual anointing of the ascended Jesus Christ.

- A false teacher often seeks to set himself up as being above his followers, often as being in an entirely separate category. The reason might be that the teacher claims to be God or a spiritual being incarnate, has some anointing from above, has been or done something in past lives or has done something in this life. A true teacher says: "The works that I do shall ye do also, and greater works shall ye do." He places attention on the students, not himself.

• A false teacher often gives himself the VIP treatment, in terms of luxury accommodations and being treated as a superior being whereas the followers and staff are living in poor conditions.

• A false teacher often creates a culture of fear in his organization so that people are afraid of questioning the leader, the teaching or are afraid of leaving.

• A false teacher often creates an organization with a double standard, leading to dishonesty. The leader and his closest associates can hide behind a smokescreen and can get away with things that are not ethical or legal.

• A false teacher often has a distinct vibration of pride and superiority that is not hard to detect—once you have been willing to look in the mirror and detect your own pride.

• A false teacher often has some character flaw or misconduct that is either hidden or explained away with some cleaver reasoning. However, nothing can justify abusing other people sexually, physically, emotionally or by taking their money.

• A false teacher often seeks to make his followers co-dependent upon him so they do not dare to make their own decisions. They do not think for themselves but ask for the guru's advice or base their decisions on the outer teaching rather than their inner Christ discernment.

• A false teacher is actually stealing the spiritual energy of his followers. He can do this by people placing their attention upon him, but for many false teachers this is not enough to give them the energy they need to survive or crave in order to build their egos. They use various forms of spiritual and emotional manipulation in order to force people to release their energy. If you feel empty or exhausted after being near a teacher that is a danger signal.

In short, we might say that a true teacher is seeking to give to the followers and raise them up. A false teacher is seeking to take from the followers and use it to raise himself up above all other people.

Let me make it clear that there is a danger in giving any kind of list to expose false teachers. The danger is that the false teachers will know what criteria I list and can counteract it. This has been going on for thousands of years on this planet, thus there are some false teachers who are extremely good at disguising themselves. There are also some true teachers who may display one or more of these characteristics. Again, only the use of intuition can give you true discernment. Which makes it essential for us to discuss how certain forces in your own psychology can interfere with your discernment.

How the ego interferes with your discernment

What I have done in the above sections is to question the way many people seek to discern between true and false teachings. An immature person will use a very black-and-white form of judgment based on outer criteria defined by the duality consciousness. It is my hope that the more mature seekers will realize that in order to develop true discernment, you need to become aware of how the ego will seek to influence the process. The purpose of spiritual growth is to transcend the ego, and you cannot do this as long as you let the ego influence your path. The ego will never take you to the promised land, but will take you into a blind alley to ensure its own survival.

The ego wants you to follow a false path, a path which promises that you can be saved without leaving behind the ego. Essentially, all false teachers promise you that they can take you on this false path, what I call the outer or mechanical path, to salvation. The result is that your ego is constantly trying to make you follow any false teacher and reject any true teacher you come across.

The ego will seek to make you believe that any idea which threatens to expose itself or its manipulation of you is a false idea. The ego will do this primarily by defining a particular false idea as beyond questioning, then saying anything which contradicts or goes beyond it is a false idea.

To understand how the ego manipulates you, you need to study all of my teachings on the ego [See the three books on the ego in the *From the Heart of Jesus* series]. However, let me give you the main thrust used by the ego. Most false teachers will promise you that they can save you, meaning that they can do the work for you that qualifies you for salvation.

By the mere act of following them — according to the rules they define — you will be saved, attain a higher state of consciousness, be whisked up by a UFO or whatever the promise might be. What they are really saying is that you can be saved without doing the hard work of looking for the beam in your own eye – the ego – and overcoming it. You can be saved without transcending the death consciousness and putting on your personal Christhood.

The ego will do everything it can to try to make you accept this claim and reject the reality that there is no substitute for self-transcendence. One example is the Christian claim that I have taken upon myself all the sins of the world. Another is the New Age claim that being kind and loving is all you need.

In seeking to cloud your discernment, your ego will skillfully use whatever unresolved issues you have in your psychology. These are the issues that make you vulnerable to a false teacher in the first place. There are many of these, but let me mention one of the most common ones. Many sincere spiritual seekers are not powerful people but are very loving people. As a result, their egos have often managed to lower their self-esteem. This makes them vulnerable to a false teacher who makes the claim that he is a very special person who can do all the work for them.

These people often feel that they can't save themselves so they need a strong leader. Once they have accepted the leader, their self-esteem gets a boost by being a follower of this "perfect" leader. However, their sense of self-esteem also depends on them following the leader rather than thinking for themselves. As long as the leader can maintain his aura of infallibility, he can get such people to do almost anything. Because they are seeking to avoid taking personal responsibility – which they feel they are not capable of doing – they will follow even the most outrageous directions from the leader.

Other people are very strong intellectually, and their egos will seek to make them feel pride over being able to understand a very complex teaching. In reality, explaining the basic dynamics of spiritual growth is not that complicated and does not require a sophisticated intellectual explanation. Some people have fallen into the trap that if a teaching is hard to understand, it must be very sophisticated.

Still other people are very emotional and the ego will use their emotions to manipulate them. This can be through fear or it can be by playing on people's anger. For example, some people live in constant fear of the end of the world or some major cataclysm, and as a result they dare not express their Christhood. They reason that only when the danger to the world is over, can they work on their Christhood. Others live in anger against another group of people or even dark forces. Their goal is to defeat the adversary rather than attaining the Christhood that enables them to transcend the adversary.

Both the ego and a false teacher will exploit whatever unresolved issues you have in your psychology. They will seek to magnify these issues – such as fear – and then use them to manipulate you in a certain direction. In many cases a false teacher doesn't know when to quit, meaning that he takes the manipulation too far and exposes himself. That is why many people eventually come to see through a false teacher.

However, it is essential for you to understand that the ego often wins either way. As long as you are following a false teacher, the ego has you going in the wrong direction. Should you come to see through the false teacher, the ego can often get people to jump into the opposite extreme of rejecting all teachers or the spiritual path as a whole. Either way, the ego has won and has managed to stay hidden from view, blaming everything on the outer teacher. My larger point here is that for you personally there really is only one false teacher, namely your ego. Any outer teacher is just an instrument that your ego uses to manipulate you and at the same time provide a scapegoat that diverts attention from the real problem—the ego itself. The main goal for the ego is to influence you while staying hidden, and it will ruthlessly exploit an outer teacher to attain this goal. It can even use a true teacher to do this by making you believe you don't have to think for yourself now that you have this perfect teacher.

Using a false teacher as a springboard for growth

When spiritual seekers come to the conclusion that they have followed a false teacher, one of the most common reactions is that they become angry at the teacher and feel they were deceived and manipulated. Such feelings are very understandable, but there comes a point where it is necessary to look beyond the feelings and ask a very important question: "Do you want to grow from the experience or do you want to allow your ego to turn it into an excuse for not taking the next step on the path?"

You see, God has created the law of karma so any false teacher will surely reap the karma for having misled you. That simply is not your concern, for God's law will take care of this and does not need your assistance. What should be your concern is how you can turn the experience with a false teacher into a step forward on your personal path. This can be done only if you are willing to take responsibility for your path, look in the mirror and ask yourself what it is in your psychology that made you vulnerable to this false teacher? Why did you believe in the promises made by the teacher, promises you now realize were empty?

If you are willing to go through this self-evaluation process – even if it is painful – you can turn the entire situation around and make great progress. If you are not willing to look for the beam in your own eye, you can spend a lifetime complaining about the splinter in the eye of another, and you will end up wasting an embodiment without making the progress called for in your divine plan. Instead, ask yourself why you were so anxious to follow a teacher who told you what your ego wanted to hear?

I know it can be painful to admit that it was your own psychological issues that made you vulnerable to the false teacher. It is far easier to accept the belief – promoted by certain sides, such as the so-called anti-cult movement – that the teacher was so skillful that he could take over your mind. The reality is that no one can take over your mind unless you allow them to do so. It is the unresolved issues in your own psychology that make you give others control over your mind. You believe in the false promise that if you give them control, they will remove issues for you so you don't have to confront them yourself.

Let me make a clear statement that can seem heartless, but is actually very liberating when you accept it: If you have followed a false teacher, there can be only one reason, namely that you have not taken full responsibility for your own path! It is the attempt to avoid taking this responsibility that caused you to give a false teacher influence over your life.

The liberating aspect of this truth is that you can use the experience with a false teacher to take the essential step that will put you beyond the reach of any false teacher. That step is that you accept full responsibility for your own path and begin to sharpen your Christ discernment and your ability to make right decisions. This is when you step away from the false path to salvation – the outer path – and step onto the true path to salvation, namely the inner path of self-transcendence, the path to personal Christhood.

You can now use your experience with a false teacher to expose your ego, instead of allowing the ego to use the experience to take you away from the spiritual path and continue hiding in the shadows of your unresolved psychology. For example, if you can honestly admit that you have a problem with low self-esteem, you can begin to reach for a true sense of self – namely that you were created as a co-creator with God – and then gradually build a true sense of self-esteem that cannot be manipulated by the ego or other people. Once you know who you are, you will not feel inferior to any person, and you no longer need a teacher who claims superiority.

Why people choose false teachers

Let us now take this to an even deeper level. Is it possible that your exposure to a false teacher is part of your divine plan? The divine plan is a blueprint for this embodiment that you made before being born. You made this plan in cooperation with your Christ self and spiritual teachers, and you made it while having a broader perspective than you have now—where you see everything from inside the mental box of your current embodiment. People often plan for things to happen that they would not have chosen while inside their current situation. Why would you choose to be exposed to a false teacher? Here are the most common reasons:

- In past lives, you have developed or have not overcome a particular weakness. You choose a false teacher who can play on this weakness as a way to force yourself to deal with it in this lifetime

- In past lives you have shown an unwillingness to take (full) responsibility for your path. You choose a false teacher to force you to deal with this issue and take full responsibility.

• In past lives you have not developed sufficient Christ discernment. You choose a false teacher to help force yourself to finally develop this discernment.

• You might have mastered the above lessons in past lives, but you now choose to demonstrate the path for others. Your intent is to allow yourself to be exposed to false teachers so you can demonstrate that they will not stop your progress. You want to demonstrate how to overcome adverse conditions and still move forward on the spiritual path.

Regardless of the motivation, the essence here is that you forget all about this as you come into embodiment. You face the situation on a blank slate. It is therefore important for you to become aware of how the ego will seek to use such a situation to stop your progress on the path. You must be determined not to let the ego manipulate you into a blind alley but to keep moving forward.

You can make things easier for yourself by pondering the saying: "When the student is ready, the teacher appears." The real question is what kind of teacher you are ready for at any given moment? The teacher you attract to you will be adapted to your state of consciousness and will reflect the kind of lessons you need to learn. When you met a false teacher, it was because that was the kind of teacher you were ready for.

This is not necessarily a negative—once you overcome the naive dream that the spiritual path should be easy and problem-free. Remember that when you formulate your divine plan, you have a broader perspective. You clearly see what lessons you need to learn, and one of the main lessons is always Christ discernment. It is a fact that even a false teacher can teach you Christ discernment—or perhaps we should say that you can learn Christ discernment by being exposed to a false teacher. For some students, being exposed to a false teacher can be the fastest way to learn certain lessons.

A true spiritual seeker will not blame him- or herself and will not look at anything with regret. You should approach everything that has happened to you as a potential for learning the important lessons on the path. By taking a positive approach and looking for the beam in your own eye, you can use a false teacher as a springboard for taking essential steps forward. This is, of course, the last thing your ego wants, which is another reason for taking this positive approach.

Forgiving false teachers

In that respect, let me call your attention to the fact that forgiveness is an essential act for all spiritual seekers. I understand that many people have been abused and hurt by false teachers, and I am in no way trying to justify the actions of such manipulators. It remains a fact that the law will return to such people what they do to others. Your concern should be how you can move forward, and you can do that only by forgiving everyone involved, including the false teacher, God and yourself. Forgiving everyone is setting yourself free to move on from the situation. Not forgiving is keeping yourself karmically and psychologically linked to the false teacher.

In that respect, let me address the issue that many seekers had an intuitive experience when they first met a false teacher. They felt an inner prompting to follow this teacher, and now that they have come to realize it was a false teacher, they feel betrayed by their intuition/inner guidance, being reluctant to trust it again. However, the intuitive prompting you got was to follow the teacher. The assumption that it was a genuine teacher was something your ego managed to project onto the situation—based on your own unresolved psychology and the dreams that followed from it. This was done for the purpose of setting you up for a fall when the illusion was punctured. Your ego wanted to make you distrust your inner guidance, which is the only way for you to reach beyond the duality consciousness.

Your inner prompting was true. It was part of your divine plan for you to follow this false teacher in order to learn certain lessons. Do not allow your ego to use the situation to get you to distrust your inner guidance and your divine plan. Learn the lesson and move on! Use the situation to expand the clarity of your inner guidance and your awareness of how the ego can distort a true direction in order to take you into a blind alley. Things are not always as they seem, and there is often a greater purpose for why you have to go through situations that might be unpleasant or seem like a mistake.

It is especially important to realize that many of the initiations on the spiritual path are subtle—especially at the higher levels. There is often a hidden lesson behind every surface appearance. For example, there can be a positive purpose behind meeting a false teacher, once you look behind the surface assumption that you should meet only true teachers. Always seek to step back from any situation and ask yourself what might be the hidden lesson.

Some people are afraid that if they could be fooled by a false teacher once, what is to prevent them from being fooled again. Some even take this to the extreme of not wanting to ever trust any teacher.

The reaction of not wanting to ever trust a teacher again comes only from the ego. It is not a true inner response so you need to see it for what it is and dismiss it. It is a valid concern that if you have been fooled once, you could be fooled again, However, this is only the case if you did not learn the lessons you needed to learn from the situation. If you did not take full responsibility for the situation, you will not have learned all of your lessons. You are likely to attract another false teacher as an opportunity to learn the unlearned lesson.

There are many people who are exposed to a false teacher and realize this, but they blame the teacher. Such people will not learn their lessons but will simply attract another false teacher. Perhaps this next false teacher takes on a completely different disguise. For example, some people have followed a false teacher in the New Age field only to submit to another false teacher in the anti-cult movement or a fundamentalist Christian church. Some people can attract several false teachers over one or more lifetimes, all the while failing to learn the lesson and accept full responsibility for their path. Once you understand the workings of the ego and are willing to look for the unresolved issues in your psychology – the issues that make you vulnerable to false teachers – you can quickly put this behind you.

Some people have a deep sense of regret, feeling they should have known better. Some even feel that their Christ self or the masters should have warned them.

The sense of regret is often reinforced by the ego in its attempt to make you distrust the spiritual path itself. However, sometimes the regret does come from a deeper part of your being because you knew that you knew better—but you allowed your ego to manipulate you into discounting your intuitive warnings. It is a fact that you will always receive a warning, but in many cases people ignore them or rationalize that they are not important. This always happens because the ego exploits your unresolved psychology, making skillful use of your expectations of what this wonderful new teacher will do for you.

You rationalize that once you have been turned into a perfect human being by the teacher, you are no longer vulnerable to the very things that the false teacher and your ego will use to manipulate you. Your regret comes from the fact that you fell for the temptation to think that the teacher would resolve your issues for you—whereas the reality is that the teacher would make them more visible so as to force you to deal with them.

Simply let go of this regret and realize that it is never too late to learn your lessons. Take responsibility for your path and move on. It is far better to admit that you made a mistake and move on than to let your ego talk you into not admitting your mistake. The latter will only keep you stuck in the state of consciousness that caused you to make the mistake in the first place. It is time to move on and self-transcend.

Some people are concerned that they might somehow have been permanently affected in a way they cannot escape.

This is a valid concern because some of the most ruthless false teachers can indeed insert a "psychic hook" into the subconscious minds of those who have submitted themselves to them. Even after you have seen through and left such a teacher, the person can still influence you and drain energy from your energy field.

While this is a often carried out with great aggressiveness on the part of the false teacher, it must be stated that no one can influence your mind against your free will. You gave the false teacher access to your mind, and you did so precisely because there were certain unresolved problems in your psychology that you were not willing to face. You fell for the promise that the teacher would do the work for you without you having to face the music.

The only way out is that you accept full responsibility for your path and resolve – perhaps with the help of a professional – the psychological issues. Once they are resolved, the false teacher will have no inroad into your consciousness— the prince of this world will come and have nothing in you. However, as an intermediate step, it can be very helpful to call forth spiritual protection and ask Elohim Astrea or Archangel Michael to cut you free from all ties to false teachers. Many of our invocations are valuable tools although no tool can be a substitute for you taking responsibility. [For all of the tools, see *www.transcendencetoolbox.com.*]

People who are vulnerable to such psychic manipulation are likely to have soul division or fragmentation. It is important to use the situation as a prompting to seek appropriate healing of such problems that have often followed you for lifetimes. Determine that this is the lifetime where you will make an all-out effort to seek wholeness and leave such divisions behind for good. The ultimate revenge against a false teacher who has hurt you is to use the experience to seek wholeness.

Accepting the nature of the path

As a final note, let me say that the spiritual path is an inner process between the Conscious You and your own higher being. Any teacher you encounter on earth – true or false – is simply an external influence. No teacher can do the work for you because the true goal of the spiritual path is that you attain oneness with your I AM Presence, and that sense of oneness can only come from within.

A teacher can either help or hinder the process, but you are always the one who must take each step. An immature spiritual seeker often assumes that a false teacher can only hinder your progress whereas a true teacher can only help you. In reality, that is not the case because everything depends on how you make use of the experience with the teacher. If you learn the lesson, sharpen your discernment and take responsibility for yourself, then an encounter with a false teacher can be a major step forward. If you think the teacher will do all the work for you, then even an encounter with a true teacher can hold you back.

Accept that the spiritual path is an inner path and that it is always up to you how you use each situation to learn your lessons. When you take this responsibility, you can turn every experience into a step forward. If you do not accept this responsibility, there is nothing I can do for you. You can continue to follow the false teachers who will promise you forever that they can do the work for you. But when you tire of this age-old game, remember me. I will always be here for those who are willing to look for the beam in their own eyes. With my help, pulling that beam is not nearly as difficult as your ego wants you to believe. Try me!

9 | THE CHALLENGE OF SPIRITUAL ORGANIZATIONS

Since I discovered the path, I have known a number of people who became emotionally attached to a particular organization or teaching. Some of them believe the organization has everything they need to make their ascension so they don't need to look for any new teachings or progressive revelation. Some believe their teaching can solve all of the world's problems so they spend their lives trying to convert everybody else. Some have, as you described, attained a comfortable position in an organization and are not willing to risk losing it.

Others seem to have invested so much in following a particular organization or teaching that they are not willing to let go of what they feel they have. They seem to be comfortable, and they are not willing to sacrifice their comfortability in order to grow further. I personally have always felt that you need to keep moving and that you can never stand still, which is what I hear you saying. Can you explain why

some people reach a point on the path that they are not willing to go beyond?

There are many reasons why people become attached to a certain outer organization, teaching or teacher and refuse to move beyond it. Behind the outer reasons is the fact that such lifestreams simply have not truly understood and internalized the basic element of the spiritual path, namely constant and never-ending self-transcendence.

Let me try to explain this by using an analogy from another book and adapt it to what we are talking about. I have said that most people on earth have descended far below the level of the Christ consciousness. We might say that they are spiritually crippled, and we can compare it to a person who has broken a leg. When you break a leg, you cannot walk until your leg has healed. You cannot simply jump right out of bed and start walking again. You need to retrain your muscles, and in order to do that you might use a set of crutches. By using the crutches, you can actually walk before you are ready to walk by your own power. The crutches obviously slow down your movement so they are only meant to be a temporary aid. When you are ready, you simply throw away your crutches and leave them behind permanently with no sense of attachment or regret. If a person becomes attached to the crutches and insists on using them after he or she is fully healed, we would obviously say the person is being immature.

When you first find the spiritual path, you cannot walk the path on your own. Most people are attracted to an outer teaching, organization or teacher who can serve as a set of crutches. As I have said, the teaching you find will match your current level of maturity and that teaching can help you reach the next level of the path. If it is a good teaching, it can help you rise to the next floor in your Father's house, as I described in the previous book. When you do reach the next level on your personal path, the teaching might not be able to take you any further. If you insist on holding on to it, it will become a set of crutches and slow down your progress on the path. What you need to do at that point is to simply throw away the crutches and reach for a higher teaching. When the student is ready, the next teacher is already waiting in the wings. Until the student consciously lets go of the old teacher and opens his or her mind, the next teacher cannot appear.

I think that is where many people get hung up. They feel their existing teaching has given them a sense of certainty and security in an insecure world, and they are not willing to let go of that security to find something higher. They are not willing to once again go into a state of flux in order to rise to the next level.

That is perfectly correct, and it brings us to an essential point about the spiritual path. You see this outpictured in my crucifixion. Many Christians have idolized me and think I was in complete control of every aspect of my life and mission. Many spiritual people have rejected this orthodox idolatry but have unfortunately ignored the true lessons of my life. What I am talking about here is the situation where I was hanging on the cross and cried out: "My God, my God, why hast thou forsaken me?" (Mark 15:34).

Those who idolize me will not consider what this really means, but it was a dramatic illustration of the basic initiation that a lifestream faces at every level of the spiritual path. As I have said, the essential problem is that people have fallen into a lower state of consciousness in which they have built a false sense of identity and a limited world view. The essence of the path is that you gradually rise to a correct sense of identity and a complete world view. You cannot simply take one giant leap from a low state of consciousness to full Christ consciousness. The reason being that this would shatter your sense of identity and you would lose all sense of who you are. This would be such a shock to you that you would likely go insane.

The spiritual path is a process whereby you gradually replace your limited sense of identity with a higher sense of who you are in God. At each stage of the path you face the basic initiation, namely that in order to accept a higher sense of identity, you have to be willing to let go of your limited sense of who you are. We might say that your limited sense of identity is an idol, a golden calf that you see as the true God. To rise higher on the path, you must be willing to abandon the golden calf and climb the mountain of God, as Moses demonstrated. The trick here is that you must do this without having any clear knowledge of where the path leads you and how it will end. You must be willing to have faith and take one step forward without having any guarantees of where the journey will take you. The spiritual path will never seem like a safe and secure journey to your outer mind and ego.

The need for security is a fear-based need that springs from the ego and the death consciousness. In order to take a step forward on the path, you must be willing to face your fears and conquer them with love. You must love something more than security, or you will not be willing to take the next step. At any level of the path, you will face the same initiation of letting go of everything you have. I understand that many people have gone through a long and arduous journey in this lifetime alone. They often feel they have made great sacrifices and that they have finally found some sense of stability and security. If that sense of security is based on any outer organization, teaching or person, it is a house built on sand (Matthew 7:26). It is an idol because true security cannot come from the things of this world. It can come only from within, and you can attain it only by manifesting the Christ consciousness. True security must be based on the rock of the Christ consciousness and not on the shifting sands of the death consciousness (Matthew 7:24).

I too had gone through a long and arduous journey before that fateful day when they nailed me to the cross. I had gradually built my faith in God, and I felt I had a certain world view that put me in control of the situation around the crucifixion. I had certain expectations and hopes of how God would save me from the cross. As I was hanging there, looking down upon the scornful crowd, I suddenly felt like the Presence of God – that had sustained me throughout my mission – left me behind. At that moment, all of my expectations for how I would be saved from the cross came tumbling down. I had to face the realty that my expectations were not correct and that God had other plans. I would not be saved from the cross but had to die on the cross without having any guarantee of what would happen next. I first went through a few moments of grief and shock. But then my faith in God came back full force, and I surrendered myself to God's will in full faith that his vision was better than my own. I then gave up the ghost (Mark 15:37), and my Conscious You lovingly left the physical body behind. It was this act of surrender on my part that opened the door to my resurrection and ascension.

I realize this is a dramatic illustration, yet it is not overly dramatic. As you rise to the higher levels of the path, you will be faced with the initiations of having to leave behind everything that got you to that point. You must literally leave behind all outer expectations and all human sense of security. You must be willing to give up everything, to lose your sense of identity, even your physical life, in order to rise to the next level of the path. Once again, consider the following saying:

"For whosoever will save his life shall lose it: and whosoever will lose his life for my sake shall find it" (Matthew 16:25). The inner meaning is that if you hold on to any aspect of your mortal life or sense of identity, you cannot make it all the way to full Christhood. You will lose that Christhood, which is the true source of life in a spiritual sense. If you seek to hold on to your mortal life, you will lose the eternal life in the Christ consciousness.

Let me make it clear that I am not hereby saying that in order to manifest Christhood you have to actually die. It is not necessary to die before you become the Christ. I very much need people to manifest their Christhood while they are still here on earth. The important point is your willingness to sacrifice everything in this world in order to reach Christhood. It is this willingness to move higher, this non-attachment to the things of this world that is the essential key to passing the initiations on the spiritual path. At the lower levels of the path, you are only required to sacrifice part of your limited sense of identity. As you reach the top, you will be required to sacrifice everything that is left of that mortal sense of identity. Only then can you accept your new identity in Christ and see yourself as a son or daughter of God. The key is to love God with all your heart so you will not stop until you attain union with God.

That is an incredible teaching, and I assume it ties in with what you said earlier, namely that any teaching or teacher can become a false teacher?

Correct, and this raises another important point. If you are following a teaching with a high degree of error, you will have to leave that teaching behind in order to manifest your Christhood.

As you grow on the path, you will eventually find a teaching that contains a high degree of truth. In that case, you might not have to leave that teaching behind in order to manifest Christhood. However, you will have to *be willing* to leave the teaching behind. You must be non-attached to the outer teaching. If you do become attached to a teaching, then that teaching – even if it is pure and has a high degree of truth – will become a false teaching. The reason being that the definition of a false teaching is any teaching that prevents you from reaching your Christhood. Even a true teaching can do that if you become attached to it.

If you transcend your attachments, you can often find a new approach to the old teaching that allows you to stay with an organization and still move on toward Christhood. The same holds true for many other situations in life, such as your family, friends or career. As we discussed earlier, you might have to leave both outer circumstances or people behind in order to rise to a new level of the path. If you can overcome your attachments, you can often stay with your outer circumstances while still moving on in consciousness. However, true non-attachment means that you are willing to move on regardless of whether you stay with certain outer circumstances. You will not allow anything in this world to prevent you from taking the next step toward Christhood. You will not allow the prince of this world to have anything in you.

Today there are so many people who claim to be taking messages or dictations from ascended masters or other beings. I know many people who get confused because the messages are often contradictory. Can you give people some guidelines for how to deal with this?

I want all spiritual seekers to become aware of their own intuition. It is not my intent to make this book or our websites a clearinghouse where people can ask questions about every spiritual movement or teaching out there. I am not interested in having people follow me through a website but having them find me in their own hearts. My intent for this external Word is to give people enough hints that they can develop their own intuition and discernment, eventually finding the internal Word.

One of the main challenges of the Piscean age was for people to overcome the tendency to blindly follow the blind leaders. The Aquarian age is meant to be an age of freedom, but you cannot be free if you do not have Christ discernment to see what is real and what is unreal. Freedom does not mean doing whatever your ego wants but rising above the ego. In order to be spiritually free, you must be able to rise above black-and-white thinking without becoming trapped in gray thinking. Let me give further thoughts that can help people sharpen their discernment.

For thousands of years it has been a divine mandate, or law, that certain spiritual truths – often called mystical, occult or esoteric knowledge – could not be revealed publicly. During my mission in Israel, I was under this law, which can be seen from the following quote:

> 33 And with many such parables spake he the word unto them, as they were able to hear it.
> 34 But without a parable spake he not unto them: and when they were alone, he expounded all things to his disciples. (Mark, Chapter 4)

The official Christian churches have always been based on the knowledge I was able to reveal publicly, primarily in my parables. Throughout the last 2,000 years (and before) the ascended masters have worked with various individuals and organizations, sometimes called secret societies, that revealed more esoteric knowledge to people who had been willing to undergo special initiations.

This was only an interim stage, for it was always our intent that all spiritual knowledge should be given freely to all people. This, however, could not – for a variety of complex reasons – come to pass until we came closer to the Aquarian age. In the Age of Freedom, it is obvious that nothing can be kept secret. All that is hidden must be made plain.

For the past 2,000 years much esoteric knowledge was not publicly available. Much of what I explain in these books and on our websites was "forbidden" knowledge until the divine mandate was changed in the 19th century. There is nothing that the human ego cannot pervert so the system of creating secret societies to disseminate esoteric knowledge was by no means ego-proof. Secrecy gives opportunity for abuse and manipulation, for the leaders of a secret society can get away with almost anything by appealing to the need to keep things secret. Likewise, the entire psychology of being in a secret society – having knowledge the general population doesn't have – encourages spiritual pride. Those who already have a tendency toward pride will have it reinforced.

Many spiritually aware people know that after the divine mandate was changed – which allowed the ascended masters to publicly disseminate esoteric knowledge – we sponsored certain organizations and messengers. However, let me give you a more nuanced understanding of what actually took place.

In order to give you this understanding, I want to correct a common misunderstanding about the early Christian movement, a misunderstanding created by the rewriting of history performed by the early Catholic Church. Consider the following quotes from Acts, Chapter 2:

> 1 And when the day of Pentecost was fully come, they were all with one accord in one place.
> 2 And suddenly there came a sound from heaven as of a rushing mighty wind, and it filled all the house where they were sitting.
> 3 And there appeared unto them cloven tongues like as of fire, and it sat upon each of them.
> 4 And they were all filled with the Holy Ghost, and began to speak with other tongues, as the Spirit gave them utterance.
>
> 16 But this is that which was spoken by the prophet Joel;
> 17 And it shall come to pass in the last days, saith God, I will pour out of my Spirit upon all flesh: and your sons and your daughters shall prophesy, and your young men shall see visions, and your old men shall dream dreams:
> 18 And on my servants and on my handmaidens I will pour out in those days of my Spirit; and they shall prophesy:

The orthodox churches of today tend to portray early Christianity as a very homogenous movement, centered around the official church. The reality was entirely different, namely that the early Christian movement was an extremely diversified movement. It was so diversified that it could hardly be called a movement by today's standards. Why was this so? As I said to Nicodemus:

> The wind bloweth where it listeth, and thou hearest the sound thereof, but canst not tell whence it cometh, and whither it goeth: so is every one that is born of the Spirit. (John 3:8)

The Holy Spirit is not something that is tightly controlled by some divine overseer. The Holy Spirit is like a rush of wind over a lake, and anyone who has a sail raised can catch it—at least for a season. The quote from Acts illustrates a general outpouring that anyone with some spiritual attunement can be part of. As quoted above: "I will pour out of my Spirit upon all flesh."

After I ascended, a portion of my Spirit was indeed poured out over this planet, and many people – all over the world – caught part of it. For example, many among my direct followers did catch it, but also many who had never met me, including many whom the Church later labeled as gnostics or heretics. This outpouring is allowed because the Holy Spirit is an opportunity for growth. How does the Holy Spirit give people the opportunity to grow? Partly by reinforcing whatever it touches!

Take note of that remark. When you catch the Holy Spirit, allowing it to flow through your being, it reinforces anything in your being, both what is of Christ and what is of anti-christ. By reinforcing everything, the Spirit makes more visible what is in your being, giving you an opportunity to let go of what is not of Christ and multiply what is of Christ.

This is an essential realization because it is the very factor that determines what actually happens to a movement. If a movement begins to form, that movement may become a conduit for a greater and more concentrated/directed flow of the Holy Spirit. This flow will increase only if both the leader(s) and the members use the Spirit's gifts to transcend themselves. A movement can start out as having a genuine flow of the Holy Spirit, but if the people do not multiply the talents they have been given, the flow of the Spirit will stop, be redirected or stall at a certain level.

What I am leading up to here is that in the late 1800s, we initiated a general outpouring of the Holy Spirit that was designed to break up the old, Piscean mindset — of blindly following the blind leaders — and clearing the way for a new Aquarian mindset where each person can have his or her personal inner connection to the spiritual realm. This outpouring is still ongoing, and any messenger or movement working with the ascended masters is part of the general flow.

In the 1800s, there were indeed a number of individuals who caught this outpouring and started various movements. Some were part of the Spiritualist movement and others developed into organizations that still exist today. There was not only one movement that had some degree of the Holy Spirit. Some movements had a more direct sponsorship by one or several masters than others, meaning that an organization can be sponsored by some ascended masters and not by others.

As I said, there has been a continuous outpouring of the Holy Spirit since the 1800s. Certainly, some organizations have had a more concentrated/directed release and some have had various degrees of direct sponsorship from the ascended masters. There always has been and always will be more than one person who is an open door for the flow of the Holy Spirit.

I am aware that some organizations have felt they had a claim to exclusivity, and they base this on what was said in dictations by us. The underlying mechanism is that in order to enter the consciousness of Aquarius, people have to leave behind – fully and finally – the entire consciousness that any human being or organization can have a monopoly on God, the ascended masters, the Holy Spirit or the Living Word. We have sometimes inflated what people wanted to believe as a test—for the messenger and the students.

What can be difficult for some students to understand is that we of the ascended masters have as our overall goal the spiritual awakening of humankind. We are constantly seeking for ways to accomplish this, and contrary to what many people think – because they have not overcome the Piscean curse of exclusivity – we are not seeking to do this through a particular organization or person. In the Aquarian age there will not be one savior or messenger but many—each person must be under his own I AM Presence.

When we inspire an organization, we have a high potential and a low potential. As an organization progresses, it will become clear whether the high potential can be reached, and if not, we cannot maintain the prior level of sponsorship. I am not saying that we make light of the sacrifices people have made within a particular organization. I am simply saying that God is no respecter of persons or the organizations to which people sometimes become loyal—rather than being loyal to our overall goal.

When we start an organization, it is not guaranteed whether the high or the low potential (or some middle ground) will be manifest. This will depend on one thing, namely to what degree the leaders and the members of an organization are willing to transcend themselves. Will people allow the Holy Spirit that flows through the organization to expose the elements of anti-christ in their beings and will they choose to leave them behind? Will people multiply the elements of Christ in their beings and dare to express their Christhood—even if it is not encouraged or welcome in the organizational culture?

What happens if we sponsor an organization and it becomes clear that the highest potential cannot be fulfilled? Even if we sponsor an organization, there is still the backdrop of the general outpouring of the Holy Spirit, and at any time people can catch this wind in their sails. It is entirely possible that some people internalize the teachings given through one organization to such a degree that they can now catch the flow of the spirit through themselves. If they are not allowed to express this in the existing organization, they must then move on and start a new initiative.

However, let me make one thing clear. In the Piscean dispensation we could give a general sponsorship of an entire organization, which meant that any member in good standing would be affected by this sponsorship. For example, we might agree to take on ourselves – for a time – a portion of the karma of each member. This was an experiment, and under the Aquarian dispensation we will only sponsor individuals. If people come together in an organized fashion, we will multiply the group's efforts, but not in the way that anyone who enters receives a certain sponsorship. From now on, at least for the foreseeable future, no one will be given sponsorship beyond what they merit based on their willingness to multiply their talents. In the Aquarian age, everyone is meant to sit under his own vine and fig tree, not under the umbrella of a spiritual master.

When a group of people come together in a positive way and are open to the Spirit, there will be an outpouring of the Holy Spirit, as happens in many Christian churches every Sunday. There are some Evangelical and Pentecostal ministers who have a certain outpouring of the Spirit, even though they seek to force the wind to flow through their fundamentalist belief system. This is allowed for a season in order to give both the minister and the congregation an opportunity to grow.

Eventually the Spirit magnifies the unresolved psychology of the minister until it surfaces, as has been the case with several well-known ministers.

It must also be noted that when a person or organization catches a general outpouring of the Spirit, there is always an interim period where people are given an opportunity to internalize the Spirit, purify their beings and rise above old momentums. This is typically a three-year grace period, and in this period a messenger can seem to have more light than the average person. What happens after the first three years depends on the degree of internalization and the willingness to rise above the old mindset—for both leaders and members.

This grace period can often be mistaken by both leaders and members as a genuine sponsorship by the ascended masters. In reality, it is a trial period, and if there is not sufficient self-transcendence, the organization will not receive a further multiplication of its efforts. One sign of the lack of such multiplication will be that an organization has light but there is little new revelation or substance in what is being brought forth. If there is not the willingness to self-transcend, how can we bring forth new revelation through a messenger or organization?

We now come to the subtle – but essential – point that mature spiritual seekers need to contemplate. There are indeed many people – even some channelers – who have a genuine outpouring of the Holy Spirit and can bring forth a flow of the Spirit that does come from the ascended masters. This is why many spiritually aware people can feel that a certain person or organization has a positive vibration or a genuine outpouring of the Spirit (obviously there are also false spirits who can show signs and wonders but do not have the vibration of the Holy Spirit). There is nothing wrong with sensing this, and it is indeed a good step toward Christ discernment to be able to sense the Spirit.

There is a higher level of discernment that can be reached only after some time and a certain amount of – sometimes difficult – experiences. This is related to the four challenges of Christ. Peter passed the first challenge, which is to recognize Christ—or recognize the Spirit. It is good to be able to recognize that some people have a flow of a higher vibration than the average preacher, who simply regurgitates from the pulpit what he was taught at seminary.

The second challenge of Christ is whether you will follow the Living Christ and transcend yourself or whether you will seek to force the Christ and his teaching into your mental box. Will you grow or will you stay where you are comfortable? Will you let the old self die in order to be reborn into a higher sense of identity? Will you follow Christ beyond your mental box or will you seek to force the Living Christ to fit into your box whereby you are left behind by Christ?

Everything is created from the interplay of the two basic forces, the expanding and the contracting force, the Father and Mother, the Alpha and Omega. The Alpha aspect of discernment is to recognize the flow of the Spirit, and the Omega aspect is to be able to discern the contents and form of that flow. The first question is whether a person, messenger or organization has a genuine flow of the Spirit. The second question is whether that flow is being used for self-transcendence or whether it is being used to cement a certain position in which people are comfortable?

As I said, it is possible that people can have a flow of the Spirit, but they are not transcending themselves. They are imposing a certain belief system upon the flow of the Spirit and the Spirit will to some degree allow this. As I said, some fundamentalist preachers do have a flow of the Spirit even though they impose their literal beliefs upon it. Likewise, a person can impose a preconceived belief system to the extent of believing he or she is taking dictations from Jesus Christ while I am not there.

Take note that I am not hereby saying such dictations are necessarily from a false spirit or impostor. I am simply saying that mature spiritual seekers need to start contemplating just how easy it is for people's minds to impose mental images upon the Spirit. The Omega side of discernment requires one to rise above the tendency to impose mental images upon the Spirit. The flow of the Spirit is like the white light that streams from the light bulb in a movie projector. The images on the movie screen are shaped by the images that are on the film strip that the light passes through—meaning the mind of the messenger and even the collective mind of the congregation.

This ability to project mental images upon the pure light of the Spirit is the main cause of many of the religious conflicts seen throughout history where two movements are sure they have the only true revelation from God. Of course, it is also this very ability that gives people the potential to serve as co-creators with God, bringing God's kingdom into manifestation on earth. It all depends on the purity of the film strip in your mind, which depends on your willingness to let the Christ expose any impurities and then let them go. The real question is whether a messenger is willing to always self-transcend or whether he or she will seek to defend a certain earthly position.

When a messenger starts out, it is allowed that the person imposes his or her mental images upon the light. If the messenger – as most messengers do – reaches a point from where he or she is not willing to go higher, then the delivery of the word will be stifled at that level. There can still be a flow of the Spirit, but the contents will not progress beyond a certain level, which means it will begin to seem like there is nothing new—which there isn't. One might conclude from this that no one is an entirely pure messenger, which is true. This does not mean that all messengers are worthless, and it is important to avoid becoming a skeptic who denies all communication from Above. You need to recognize that communication is possible without becoming attached to any particular expression, and you do that by always seeking to raise your ability to experience the Spirit of Truth directly. Even if an organization has an imperfect expression of the Spirit, it does show that there is something beyond the "normal" state of consciousness, beyond the material realm. If you keep following the flow toward its source, you will eventually encounter the source itself. In the Aquarian age, the essential step for humankind is to recognize that it is possible to receive communication from the spiritual realm and that everyone has that potential—if they are willing to engage in the process of perpetual self-transcendence.

When we of the ascended masters evaluate an organization, we look beyond outer details—including erroneous claims made by the organization. We do not demand that leaders or members should be perfect, we look at the net gain produced by an organization. For example, does the organization help people transcend themselves—even if not to the maximum potential? Does the organization release more positive than negative energy into the planetary energy field? Take note again that an organization being a net gain does not mean it has any direct sponsorship. I am talking about the leaders and members being able to catch the general outpouring of the Spirit and multiplying it to some degree.

For a time, a spiritual seeker might benefit from being involved with such an organization. But if you are transcending yourself, there will come a point where you seriously need to consider whether you will continue in that environment—and you especially need to be aware of misguided loyalty to anything in this world. As we always say, when the student is ready, the teacher appears. The problem is that until you are willing to leave your nets – where you are comfortable – the Living Christ cannot appear and call you to become a fisher of men. As long as you hold on to an organization because you feel the Spirit but not the substance, you will not be able to see the next teacher who can give you the higher substance. How should you evaluate the contents of a teaching? Here are a few pointers as food for thought:

- Does the teaching bring forth something that is genuinely new. A particular organization is designed to bring forth a certain teaching for a certain level of consciousness. An organization is meant to bring forth teachings within a certain framework (not the ultimate teaching for the Aquarian age, as there is no such teaching). Another messenger may pick up that torch and bring forth a more detailed teaching within the same framework, but it has to be beyond what was already given. Otherwise, it will not be released from the ascended masters but will be the messenger imposing his or her belief system upon the flow of the Spirit.

- At some point a new messenger must go beyond the old teaching and bring forth more than was given in the old. Otherwise, the movement will stall and rise no higher.

- Does the teaching challenge you to come up higher or does it make you comfortable where you are? As I said, people can catch the Spirit, and some messengers have even had a more direct sponsorship for a time, but if they do not multiply their talents and self-transcend, the sponsorship will be withdrawn and the Spirit will now stay within certain boundaries, defined by what people are unwilling to surrender. The flow of the Spirit might continue, but the teachings are no longer coming from the ascended masters. They might come from a person's higher self, from the collective consciousness of the members or from beings in the mental or emotional realm. Some of these beings might indeed be impersonating ascended masters. One might even say that the Holy Spirit is always a transcending Spirit so if a person or organization is not self-transcending, it is no longer the Holy Spirit but a lesser spirit. Some messengers can lose the Holy Spirit but because they are not willing to give up their outer position, they become open to a lower Spirit and some of the followers cannot tell the difference.

• Does the teaching make sense? Is it consistent? Is it useful or does it simply regurgitate words. Is it all fluff – perhaps with flowering words – but has no substance? A complete teaching will have both the vibration of the Spirit and genuine content—it will have the fullness of Alpha and Omega.

• Is the teaching practical. Does it help you transform your daily life and solve some of the problems you face in the modern world, which is in many respects more complex than any previous time?

• Are the leaders walking their talk in terms of embodying the teachings? This does not mean people have to be perfect. But it does mean they have to be wiling to continually transcend themselves, which includes admitting one's imperfections and surrender-

ing them (doing whatever psychological healing work
is necessary to accomplish this).   ✗

There is an Alpha and an Omega side to progressive revelation. The Alpha is that new, more advanced teachings are
released, teachings that could not be released earlier, either
because of divine mandate or because humankind's consciousness was not ready for them. We give revelation today that
builds upon but goes beyond what was released in the past.
The Omega aspect is that we make our teachings more easily accessible and understandable for a broader audience. This
means teachings are explained in a more direct and straightforward way, often using a more normal form of language.

As an example of the progression in the delivery of the
word, you will see that the language and the concepts released
in the past were very difficult to understand, often because they
were deliberately expressed in an ambiguous way with complex
language. This can be a restriction imposed by the messenger,
either because of his/her ability/inability to use words or the
messenger's clarity of mind (or lack of it). It takes a very clear
and neutral mind to express complex concepts in a way that is
easy to understand whereas as clouded mind can express concepts only in a clouded language.

Today, humankind has risen beyond the level of awareness
they had a century ago so we can now speak in a way that is far
more direct and unambiguous—although we still leave certain
things unsaid in order to give room for people's individual discernment. There are some who prefer the old ways and think
that the harder a teaching is to understand, the more sophisticated it must be. However, remember what I said earlier about
secret societies giving rise to pride over having a teaching that
the general population does not have.

There are also some people who wonder how much more revelation we have to bring forth, sometimes believing in the claim that a certain organization has brought forth some ultimate teaching. I can assure you that the amount of progressive revelation that we can bring forth is unlimited. Progressive revelation is progressive precisely because it never stops. We have many more things to say and we have many new ways of describing timeless truths in order to make them easier to grasp for people in this particular time.

In reality, the most sophisticated spiritual teaching is the one that can be grasped and internalized by the greatest number of people. We are beyond the age of elitism so we are looking for messengers who can express truth in a clear, unambiguous and straightforward manner. We are looking for students who can appreciate this and become part of spreading the word to as many people as possible—changing the entire tone of the religious debate.

We of the ascended masters were never in the consciousness of elitism—although many of our students have been and continue to be. It is time to leave those nets behind and become fishers of men in the Aquarian waters—in which the secret of life is given to all who have ears to hear.

10 | THE FEAR-PRIDE DYNAMIC

You are talking a lot about discernment. Some people say that as we climb the spiritual path, the initiations we encounter become more difficult and subtle, and it becomes easier to get stuck. Do you agree?

It is correct that the initiations become more subtle. At the lower stages of the path, you give up your outer beliefs about the world and your own abilities. As you grow in maturity, you need to give up the deeper beliefs about how you see yourself and God. Because such beliefs are a deeper part of your identity, it can be more difficult to see them as limited or incorrect. Because they have been a part of your identity for a long time, it can be more difficult to leave them behind. You might fear that if you give up such deep beliefs, you will have no security left and will be in a state of chaos or in a vacuum. However, this fear only assails those who have not yet established a clear connection to their Christ selves. Through that connection, you will know that you will not be left in a vacuum.

Another factor is that as you grow toward Christ consciousness, you become more of a threat to the dark forces. As I said earlier, these forces are always seeking to control the population and they do so through the lies spread by the false teachers. These forces will do everything in their power to prevent you from manifesting your Christhood, and the closer you get, the more they will attack you.

There is also a saving grace. The further you go on the path, the better you can invoke light for your protection. The dark forces can only control people through the dualistic lies that spring from the death consciousness. When you attain contact with your Christ self, you can easily see through such lies and you refuse to be controlled by them.

A Christed being will not remain passive or silent but will expose the serpentine lies to other people. Thereby, you become the ultimate threat to the dark forces, and they will use all of their tricks in an attempt to ensnare you. Consequently, all spiritual seekers need to recognize that false teachers do exist and that they have one main goal, namely to prevent anyone from attaining Christhood here on earth. As I said earlier, they will use ignorance, fear and intimidation to prevent people from discovering the path and following it. As you climb the path, their tactics change slightly. They will now seek to fool you into stopping your path before you reach full Christhood. They will do this by seeking to make you believe in one of the subtle lies that can take you into a blind alley. Many of these lies play upon people's pride.

At the lower levels of the path, the false teachers seek to stop people through fear. As you rise above this threat, the false teachers become more subtle, and they now seek to ensnare you through pride. There are numerous lies that seek to stop your growth by appealing to pride, such as the idea that you have everything you need in an outer teaching, that you already know everything and don't need to learn any more, that you are so highly evolved that you don't need to give up certain limited beliefs or go through certain humiliating situations or that you are so sophisticated that you have already overcome the ego.

Fear and pride are two sides of the same coin, and they both spring from ignorance—or more specifically from partial knowledge. All fear is a fear of the unknown because you fear that which you know or suspect exists but do not understand. Once you understand a threat, you also know how to deal with that threat. Pride comes in when you have attained more knowledge but not yet the full knowledge of life. You now begin to feel that because you know so much and have gone through so much on the path, you have passed a certain point and you are above and beyond the initiations of the path.

I was given the test of pride by the devil after my fasting in the wilderness (Matthew 4:1-11) and by Peter when I told my disciples I would have to suffer. He thought I was above this, and I rebuked him sternly because it was the false teachers of this world that were speaking through him at that moment (Matthew 16:21-26). Thereby, I demonstrated that no one is above being tested on the path and that we all have to pass the test of humility before we can manifest Christhood.

When you have attained some knowledge of the path, it is very tempting to feel that you have somehow risen above other people and that you are now more important in the eyes of God. God is no respecter of persons (Acts 10:34), and the reason is that God knows that all life is one. Is one drop in the ocean better than another drop? Only ignorance can cause a person to believe that he or she is more important than other people.

As you climb the path, pride becomes a very subtle force that will follow you as long as you are here on earth. A true seeker must continually be alert to the subtle temptations of pride. Because pride is so subtle, it is often unrecognized or misunderstood. It is the pride you do not see that will get to you. This is another reason why it is so essential to build discernment.

Your Christ self is above all pride and it can instantly set you straight about pride. However, it can do so only when you ask and when you are open to seeing through your prideful beliefs. You must be willing to surrender those beliefs and surrender the outer will of the ego to the greater will of the I AM Presence within you. It is this total surrender to a higher will and a higher vision that I demonstrated on the cross. You cannot make it to the top of the spiritual path without going through that total surrender.

How can we overcome pride?

You cannot overcome pride through the duality of the death consciousness and the ego so you must reach for something beyond that state of mind. You can overcome pride only by listening to a teacher who is outside your mental box, outside the bubble of your personal pride. That teacher might be your Christ self, your personal ascended master or it might be a person that appears in a humble disguise but still represents the true teacher. When the student is ready, the teacher appears. When you are trapped in pride, there is always a teacher present who can help you overcome that pride. Unfortunately, the nature of pride makes it very difficult for people to recognize the teacher because they think a true teacher must live up to certain outer requirements.

It is a sad fact that many people on the spiritual path are trapped in spiritual pride. They feel that because they are so advanced on the path, they only need to listen to teachers who meet their approval and seem to be above them. In reality, the teacher that is best suited to helping you overcome pride is the teacher who appears in a humble disguise. The trick is that in order to recognize the teacher, you have to look beyond your pride, and that is more than half the victory.

Consider the old saying: "If the messenger be an ant, heed him!" Your spiritual teacher will not always appear as some enlightened spiritual being. Learn to look for the teacher in disguise and learn to look for truth wherever it might be found. It is not the appearance of the teacher that is important—it is the truth of his teaching. If you are attached to outer appearances, you will often overlook the teacher.

How can we get to a point where we are no longer faced with the temptations of the false teachers?

By ascending to the spiritual realm. Right now, the false teachers are allowed to be on earth because the consciousness of humankind is still at a fairly low level. You will be surrounded by lies as long as you are in this world. Once you attain Christ consciousness, you will be able to easily see through the temptations of the false teachers, yet you will still encounter them on a daily basis. Your job as a Christed being on earth is to serve as a true teacher and help people rise above the lies. This will require you to deal with the lies on an ongoing basis.

How do you rise above the lies? By loving truth more than any lies, no matter how convenient and true these lies seem to your ego. When you love God and truth, you simply cannot be satisfied by a lie, and you will not rest until you have found a higher understanding that will replace all lies, as light replaces darkness.

As the consciousness of humankind continues to be raised, there will eventually come a point when the lifestreams who serve as representatives of the false teachers will no longer be allowed to embody on this planet. We will eventually clear the astral realm so that even the dark forces that reside there will be removed. We can then clear the mental and the etheric realms from the lies of the false teachers, and eventually the earth will begin to radiate spiritual light and become a spiritual sun.

What can we do to help purify the earth?

The most important task is to demonstrate that there is an alternative to the dualistic state of consciousness. The main problem on this planet is the mental images that people have built, images that limit what people think a human being can or should do. One of the most important functions of a Christed being is to demonstrate that it is possible to live without being limited by these mental boxes.

You will see that I often shocked the Jews by not living up to their expectations of how the messiah should be. It was part of my mission to help people see beyond their human expectations and see the reality of Christ. As you attain Christhood, it becomes part of your mission as well. It must come from within. You cannot fake Christhood, and you cannot teach it on an intellectual basis. You can either *be* the Christ or not be the Christ. The best thing you can possibly do to improve conditions on this planet is to be the Christ right here on earth, right now in this age.

11 | RISE ABOVE THE ENEMY WITHIN

You have talked a lot about the death consciousness and the ego. I know you have described various aspects of these inner enemies, but I am wondering if you could give a more detailed description?

The Conscious You is like a planet orbiting the sun of the I AM Presence. The ego and the death consciousness form a moon that is placed between the Conscious You and the sun so that it eclipses the light from your I AM Presence. The task of a spiritual seeker is to remove this obstruction so the Conscious You can once again be bathed in the light of your Presence.

When your lifestream was created by your spiritual parents, they gave you a unique individuality that is permanently anchored in your spiritual self. No matter what mistakes you might have made in the material universe or what beliefs you might have accepted with your outer consciousness, nothing has altered or damaged your God-given individuality. The Conscious You is an extension of your I AM Presence. It allows you to experience another level of God's creation and express your God-given individuality in the material universe.

As long as the Conscious You maintains a conscious contact with the I AM Presence, it will be expressing its God-given individuality. Although your individuality cannot be damaged, you can expand and build upon that foundation, and you are meant to do so. As the Conscious You gains experiences during its journey through God's creation, including but not limited to the material universe, you can build upon your original individuality. In co-creating with God, you are co-creating yourself.

The Conscious You was never designed to exist alone; it was designed as an extension of the spiritual self. When the Conscious You descends into the lower state of consciousness, it loses its direct contact with the I AM Presence. The Conscious You experiences this as a great loss, and because it cannot bear to be alone, it builds a pseudo identity, often referred to as the human ego. This ego sits between the Conscious You and the spiritual self. It acts as a filter or even as a barrier between your conscious mind and your spiritual self.

As explained earlier, everything in the world of form is sustained by a stream of God's light. This light is undifferentiated, but when it enters your lifestream, it is filtered through the God-given individuality anchored in your spiritual self. Your individuality acts as a prism that colors the pure light of God. This is not a degradation of the light of God. Your spiritual self simply expresses the light of God without degrading that light. When the Conscious You has conscious contact with the spiritual self, it can express the light of God in the material universe without degrading the light. You become an open door for the light of God to enter this world in a pure, but individualized, form.

The human ego, or anti-self, is created from the energies of the material world. The very nature of the ego is that it is not in alignment with your God-given individuality. It was created only because the Conscious You lost contact with the I AM Presence. If the Conscious You had maintained that contact and expressed its God-given individuality, the ego would never have been created. One might say that the concept of original sin can apply to the ego. It was created, or conceived, in imperfection—meaning separation from God.

When the light from your I AM Presence passes through the filter of the ego, it becomes degraded. As mentioned earlier, the vibration of the light falls below a certain level and becomes a sin. When the Conscious You becomes enveloped in the ego, virtually all of the energy flowing through the soul vehicle (your four lower bodies) is misqualified and falls below that critical level of vibration. One might say that there is a standard, namely the Christ standard. When you act in harmony with God's laws, the energy expressed by you will always be above a certain level of vibration. If you express energy through the lower consciousness, the vibration of the energy will be below the critical level.

Does this relate to Mother Mary's teachings where she talks about a figure-eight flow between the I AM Presence and the Conscious You?

It does. As I said, human beings were designed to be co-creators with God. When you are fulfilling this role, you are receiving God's energy through your spiritual self. The energy becomes qualified by your God-given individuality but it stays above the critical level of vibration, and it can flow back to the spiritual realm. There is a figure-eight flow between the Conscious You and the spiritual self.

When you send energy back to God, God will multiply that energy, and you will receive more energy in return. That is the principle behind planting seeds. You plant only one grain of wheat, but you receive many in return. When you multiply the energy you receive from God, you will be rewarded. "For whosoever hath, to him shall be given, and he shall have more abundance" (Matthew 13:12).

If you express God's energy through the ego, the energy will fall below the mark, and it cannot ascend back to the spiritual realm. You are, so to speak, burying your talents, meaning God's energy, in the ground, meaning the material world. When you are not sending anything back to God, there is nothing to multiply. When your lifestream first chose to descend into the material world, you were sent here with a certain portion of God's energy. This was your "talents" given to you by God. One might say that God gave you seed money but it was not a blank check. If you spend it unwisely, you will not receive any more. God will only multiply what is used in harmony with his laws. If a lifestream misuses its free will and begins to qualify energy below a certain vibration, it cannot receive additional energy from God. A lifestream can eventually spend all of its inheritance until it receives just enough energy to stay alive (Luke 15:11-32).

If you want to make progress on the path, you must bring something to the altar of God. You must bring an offering of energy that is qualified in harmony with the laws of God. Your Conscious You can only produce such energy through the guidance of your Christ self. Only that which is produced through Christ consciousness, and therefore vibrates above the critical level, will be the acceptable offering to bring to the altar of God.

What exactly does it mean that the lower state of consciousness is relative or dualistic?

When the Conscious You has contact with the I AM Presence, it is God-centered. It has an absolute standard based on the principles that God used to create this universe. I think it should be obvious that when you act in harmony with those principles, everything you do will serve to enhance your own life and the lives of those around you. Your thoughts, feelings and actions spring from an absolute standard, namely a standard that is not created by the lower mind but by a higher being, meaning God and your spiritual self.

When the Conscious You loses contact with the I AM Presence, it no longer has access to this absolute standard or guiding rod. You now build the pseudo identity, the human ego, and this identity is by its nature separate from God. The ego is built from the energies found in the material universe. It is based on a state of consciousness that does not have an absolute guiding rod. This is what is described in the Bible as the tree of the knowledge of good and evil (Genesis 2:9), meaning relative good and evil. The tree or fruit is a metaphor for a state of consciousness that has no absolute standard for right and wrong, good and evil.

From God's viewpoint, the question is simple: "Is it in harmony with the laws of God, or is it outside those laws?" When you have contact with your spiritual self, you don't think in terms of good and evil. Your only concern is whether something is of God or not of God. You have no value judgment according to which something is good or bad. When you descend into the lower consciousness, you no longer have an absolute standard.

Instead, you have a relative standard. This relative standard is based on a scale that has two opposites. You might call them good or evil, right or wrong or anything else you desire. The name doesn't matter; what matters is that anything on the scale is defined by its relationship to the opposing polarity. Something is either good or bad or somewhere in between but it is never outside the scale.

When you are caught in the lower consciousness, you think the concepts of good and evil are real and that your definition of good and evil is absolute, even infallible. You think the relative scale is the only way to look at life and that everything must somehow fit on the scale. You assign reality to good and evil; you think good and evil are objective realities. You are simply not open to the fact that both your definition of good and your definition of evil can be out of touch with the reality of God. Even that which you think is good might be in violation of the laws of God. You cannot or will not see that in order to find truth, you need to look beyond the relative scale and the entire dualistic consciousness.

When you rise above the lower consciousness and begin to attain Christ consciousness, you realize the unreality of the entire relative scale and the dualistic state of consciousness. You realize that if something is in harmony with the laws of God, it is real. If something is outside of those laws, it is not real. It does not truly exist; it has no permanent reality. One might say that what is created in harmony with the laws of God has permanent existence. What is created outside the laws of God has no permanent existence. It was created by a conscious being in a lower state of consciousness, and it can continue to exist only as long as conscious beings in that state of consciousness choose to focus their attention on this imperfect image. The very moment people take their attention off the imperfect image, it will begin to break down because it has no reality of its own. As described earlier, the second law of thermodynamics will cause all imperfect structures to break down and self-destruct.

This is hard to understand for us mere mortals!

I realize that what I am saying will make absolutely no sense to a lot of people. It is virtually impossible to use words to explain the reality of God to people in the lower state of consciousness. When you are trapped in duality, you cannot see beyond it, and you cannot grasp something that does not fit into the dualistic view of the world. That is why so many people have associated good with God and evil with the devil. In reality, God is not good according to some relative, human standard. God is beyond the relative standard by which good is defined as the opposite of evil. God has no opposite. God simply *is*.

You cannot understand the reality of God's being through the relative faculties of the emotions and the intellect. For ages, people have attempted to create philosophies that will explain reality in a way that is comprehensible to the human intellect. This simply cannot be done because they inevitably create what the Old Testament calls a graven image (Exodus 20:4). This is not simply a painting or sculpture, but even a mental image based on the relativity of the human intellect. If you want to know the reality of God, you must go beyond the dualistic state of consciousness, including the intellect. This can only be done through the Christ consciousness whereby you reach beyond the relative, dualistic state of mind.

One interpretation of the cross is that the vertical bar of the cross represents a person's ability to reach beyond the lower consciousness and reach for the Christ consciousness. The horizontal bar represents the relative scale of good and evil. When you are crucified, you are held in a fixed position by

the horizontal bar of the cross. You will remain paralyzed in
that position until you resolve the enigma represented by the
horizontal bar, the dualistic state of consciousness in which
everything is seen in relation to two polarities, none of which
represent the reality of God. To resolve that enigma, you
must go beyond the horizontal approach to life, take a vertical
approach and reach for the Christ consciousness.

Speaking of this, another important spiritual symbol is a
pyramid or triangle. The triangle can be said to represent the
spiritual path. The base line of the triangle represents the horizontal, relative state of consciousness. At one end of the line
you have relative evil, and at the other end you have relative
good. When you are moving away from God – when you are
descending the staircase – you are making the triangle bigger
and increasing the length of the baseline. You are increasing
the gap between relative good and evil. That is what the devil
and all beings who rebel against God's law have been doing for
a long time. By going further and further into the extremes of
duality, they increase the distance between relative good and
evil. The greater the gap between relative good and evil, the
harder it becomes for people to see beyond the two extremes.
One might say that when you are moving away from God,
you are expanding the base line of the triangle. The question is
how far a lifestream is willing to go before it realizes the futility
of this and decides to turn around and move in the opposite
direction.

The key to success on the spiritual path is to realize that the
truth is not found in either of the relative extremes. The truth
is not found on the base line of the triangle. Instead, the truth
is found by following the Middle Way that goes through the
tip of the triangle. Contrary to popular belief, the Middle Way
is not a compromise between good and evil. The Middle Way

is outside of, above and beyond, the relative conflict between good and evil.

As a visual symbol of this, draw a vertical line in the center of a triangle. When you follow the Middle Way, you are climbing the vertical line in the center of the triangle. Imagine that you start at the base line of the triangle and that this line represents your present level of consciousness. The base line is quite long, meaning that there is a huge difference between the extremes of relative good and evil. As I said before, a lifestream cannot suddenly leave behind the dualistic state of consciousness because it would be left in a vacuum. The key to walking the spiritual path is to gradually decrease the distance between relative good and evil. As a visual example, imagine that you rise to a higher point on the center line of the triangle. If you draw a new base line from that point, the line will be shorter than the original base line. The gap between relative good and evil has become smaller, and it has now become easier to remain centered on the Middle Way instead of being pulled into one of the extremes.

As you move forward on the path and begin to attain a more direct contact with your Christ self, you will no longer be pulled into the relative extremes of good and evil. Instead, you will gain a more balanced perspective on life, and eventually you will begin to see beyond all relativity. You begin to see the vertical truth of God instead of the horizontal world view that springs from the lower state of consciousness. As you climb the spiritual path, you ascend to the top of the triangle, to the top of the pyramid of life. What is at the very top? It is a single point. When you reach that point, you have reached the singularity of the Christ mind. You have risen beyond the duality of the lower mind with its opposite polarities. You see only the one truth of the one reality of the one God. You no longer see yourself as separated from God but as an extension of God. You are as Above, so below.

Remember my statement: "The light of the body is the eye: if therefore thine eye be single, thy whole body shall be full of light" (Matthew 6:22). So many people have been baffled by this statement. You can now see what it means. When your vision is undivided, meaning that it has risen above the relative extremes, your entire being will be filled with the light of God, the light of Christ. You will be a light onto the world, a light that is set on a hill (Matthew 5:14), the apex of the pyramid of life.

To reach that point, and to let the light of your God-given identity shine as a beacon into the darkness of the lower consciousness, is the true desire of the Conscious You. Before you came into embodiment, you desired to reach that state of Christ consciousness and thereby serve as a lighthouse that can guide your brothers and sisters to the safe harbor of the Christ consciousness. Dare to recognize your innermost desire. Dare to climb the staircase inside the pyramid of self. Dare to reach the top and enter into the singularity of union with your I AM Presence, union with God. Dare to let your light shine and do not hide it before others (Matthew 5:16), even if they persecute you for my sake (Matthew 5:11).

Are you hereby saying that many of the activities that we define as being good are not necessarily good according to the Christ standard?

That is correct. For example, many religious people – including many Christians – define a set of outer rules for how a good person should behave. Some of these rules are defined by the relativity of the death consciousness. Many people have spent a lifetime working according to such outer rules, and they often believe they have been so good that God simply has to save them. If they have not risen above the duality of the ego, they have not qualified for their salvation, no matter how good they think they are according to a man-made standard. That is why I said that unless your righteousness exceeds the righteousness of the scribes and Pharisees, you cannot make it to Heaven (Matthew 5:20).

> **That will be a tough pill to swallow for a lot of religious people. I am sure some will say that it sounds like it doesn't matter whether we are good or not.**

Yes they will, and the reason is that they are still thinking with the dualistic mind. In order to qualify for your salvation, or ascension, you need to attain Christ consciousness. In order to do that, you need to rise above the duality of the death consciousness. It is this duality that causes people to accept the concepts of relative good and evil, thinking that if they do relative good, they will automatically be saved. Doing relative good simply is not enough to get you to Heaven—you must transcend all duality, even relative good.

However, it is important to understand that doing relative good will still help you move forward on the path. If a person is doing evil works, for example committing crimes or killing other people, that person is obviously making a more severe karma than a person who is living a life according to Christian ideals. By doing good – even if it is according to a relative standard – you are still progressing on the path. The problem is that doing relative good can become a trap if you think it is all you have to do.

Many Christians have been sincerely striving to live a good Christian life, thinking this is all they have to do. When such lifestreams die, they realize that this simply isn't enough and that they have been following the way that seems right unto a man, but the ends thereof are the ways of death (Proverbs 14:12). Unfortunately, this causes some of these lifestreams to become angry, and they often come into their next embodiment with an anger against orthodox religion and Christianity. This can cause them to abandon all spirituality, and this is exactly what the false teachers want. The way out of this is to transcend all relativity and duality and strive to put on the mind of Christ.

> **Many years ago, I had a very profound experience that helped me understand this point. I met a man who had served for 30 years as a Christian missionary in a very poor part of Africa. One day he became ill and was not expected to live until the next morning. He took stock of his long life as a missionary and ended up feeling that, considering all he had done for God, he ought to be ready for his salvation. At that moment, he heard a powerful inner voice say to him something to the effect that he had only paid his dues.**
>
> **This caused quite an awakening of his soul, and he realized the fallacy of thinking it was enough to do relative good. He realized there was a deeper meaning to your life and message that he had never understood, and this gave him a strong desire to live on and internalize your message. During the night, his illness subsided and he lived on for many years with an entirely new appreciation of what it means to be a Christian.**

✗

You are privileged to have met a beautiful lifestream who had been trapped in orthodoxy for many years but was willing to transcend it. The real lesson here is that when you begin the spiritual path, you might have a motivation that is partly or fully based on the duality of the death consciousness. For example, many spiritual seekers have a desire to feel that they are more spiritually advanced than other people or that they are doing an important job for God and helping to save the planet. This is not necessarily wrong because a lifestream must start the path at whatever level of consciousness it is at when it discovers the path.

As the lifestream climbs the path, it must refine its motivation for walking the path. You must gradually leave behind all human motivation, especially all pride or a desire to be thought wise in this world (Luke 16:15). Such a motivation can easily become pride and take you into a blind alley that slows down or aborts your growth. In the end, you must rise to the point where your only motivation is love. You might love people and have a sincere desire to help them find a better way to live. You might love yourself and have a sincere desire to be all you can be. There is nothing wrong with loving yourself, as long as you love your spiritual self and see your Self as God. You might love a spiritual master and have a sincere desire to serve that master. For example, many Christians have a strong love for me or Mother Mary and a sincere desire to help make our missions successful. Even the love for such outer things can become a diversion, and in the end you need to come to a point where you walk the path for one reason only, namely that you love God with all your heart, soul and mind (Matthew 22:37).

At that point, you have moved out of fear and into love, and you now become the open door for the unconditional love of God to be present in this world. That is the truest and most valuable service you can give to God and to other people—to be the Presence of Love in this world.

You have mentioned before that the ascended masters have sponsored several organizations to bring forth new spiritual teachings. Some of those teachings talk about the dweller on the threshold. Is the dweller just another name for the carnal mind or is it more like the ego?

The concept of the dweller on the threshold is comparable to the human ego. The carnal mind can be described as a computer designed to run the physical body. However, the term "carnal mind" can also be used as a general name for the entire conglomerate of the human consciousness, which includes the ego. That is how it was used by Paul.

The expression "the dweller on the threshold" refers to the process of the lifestream deciding to hide from God. As a result of separating itself from God, from the spiritual self, the Conscious You started a process of gradually walking further and further away from God, meaning that the lifestream descended into successively lower states of consciousness. For each time the lifestream descended to a lower level, the Conscious You made a decision that caused, and seemingly justified, that descent. When the lifestream starts the spiritual path and begins to reverse the process of walking away from God, the Conscious You must face and undo each decision that caused it to descend to its current level of consciousness.

Let me illustrate this by, once again, comparing the spiritual path to a staircase in a building. One section of the staircase leads from a given floor to the next floor, which is a plateau from which the staircase goes to the next floor. Each section can be compared to one level on the spiritual path so each level has several smaller steps.

When the lifestream starts the spiritual path, it is at the level to which it descended before it turned around. It now

ascends each of the smaller steps that lead it to the next floor.
Each step represents a certain state of consciousness, a certain
decision and an amount of misqualified energy. Each step is
relatively easy to overcome. When the lifestream stands on the
uppermost step and is ready to move on to the next level of
the path (the next section of the staircase), the Conscious You
must face the original decision that caused it to descend below
that level of the path. That decision is what is called the dweller
on the threshold. It is that part of your ego that was born from
your decision to descend below that level, and it is waiting on
the threshold to your ascent from that level. Before the Conscious You can take that final step and ascend to a higher level
of the path, it must face its previous decision and undo that
decision.

If the Conscious You adopts a systematic approach to the
spiritual path and is willing to surrender itself to the higher will
of the spiritual self, surrendering the dweller will not be all that
difficult. Once you have transmuted the misqualified energy
and overcome any minor decisions made on that level, all that
is left is to undo the final decision. However, if the Conscious
You does not realize the need to overcome this decision – if it
does not recognize why the decision was limiting – the Conscious You might fail to undo the decision. If the Conscious
You has not truly understood the need to surrender every
aspect of the ego, it might tie in to the entire momentum of
its rebellion against God. Instead of having to undo only one
small part of the ego, or dweller, it now has to battle the entire
momentum, which is often overpowering. The Conscious You
cannot take that final step onto the next level, and it can indeed
become stuck and perhaps even begin to slide back down the
staircase.

The dweller on the threshold is a valuable concept, especially when it is understood to be a decision that stands in the

way of the lifestream's progress. The Conscious You can overcome the dweller only by fully recognizing what the decision entails and why it was limiting. It must then make a conscious choice to replace the imperfect decision with a right decision. Obviously, each aspect, or layer, of the dweller must be undone before the Conscious You has its final victory.

The ego would then be at the top of the staircase, as the first decision that caused a lifestream to turn its back upon God and begin descending the staircase?

Correct. In the previous book I gave the image that when you accept an imperfect belief, it is like throwing a rock into the stream of consciousness. I also said that an essential part of the path is to systematically remove these incorrect beliefs from your mind. As you remove the rocks from your stream, you will gradually uncover one large boulder that is the very first rock that was thrown into your stream. That boulder is the human ego, yet instead of merely obstructing the flow of water, the ego is so big that it actually diverts the stream of consciousness and takes it in a downward direction. In order to take the final step to Christhood, you must uncover the ego, realize that it began with an imperfect decision and consciously choose to replace that decision with a better one.

This will happen gradually if you engage in the path, as I have described in these books. You will gradually build a momentum of seeing through all wrong beliefs and incorrect decisions, and you will become much better at overcoming them without pain. It will be helpful to be aware that the ego exists and that it will be the final challenge on the path. We give important teachings on this in several other books that describe the ego. Let me give a few thoughts here.

Let us begin by looking at the ideal scenario. Your I AM Presence is a spiritual being that exists in a higher realm. At some point in the distant past, your I AM Presence decided that it wanted to experience the material universe from the inside and it wanted to help co-create the kingdom of God on planet earth. Your I AM Presence created an extension of itself that was able to descend into the lower vibrations of the material world. This is what became your Conscious You.

As I said earlier, your Conscious You was not meant to be alone; it was meant to be a planet orbiting the sun of your I AM Presence. We might say that your I AM Presence desired to build a castle on earth. It acted as the architect and the structural engineer, designing the castle and making sure the construction was sound, meaning it was in harmony with the laws of God. It then sent a part of itself, the Conscious You, to earth to serve as the artisan who would actually build the castle. The Conscious You was meant to retain its inner contact with the I AM Presence so that it could receive the blueprint for the castle directly from the source. Thereby, the Conscious You would be able to build the castle without having the full knowledge of the laws of God that is anchored in the Presence. It is like a craftsman who doesn't have an engineering degree, yet can build a house by using a blueprint from the engineer.

It might sound as if the Conscious You is just a slave of the I AM Presence, but that is only true for young lifestreams. The Conscious You has free will and it has the spark of light within it. This spark of light is a small replica of the God-flame from which the I AM Presence sprang. In some esoteric teachings, it is called the threefold flame because it embodies the qualities of power, wisdom and love. However, for each Conscious You these qualities have a unique combination that gives it self-awareness as an individual. When a Conscious You first descends, it is meant to follow the blueprint given to it by the I AM Presence, but it still has freedom to decide many of the details of the building. One might say that within the over-all framework of the blueprint, the Conscious You can decide many of the construction details and the decor of the castle.

By exercising its free will within a safe framework, the Conscious You will never go against the laws of God. This does not mean that all of its decisions will be perfect, but it does mean that the Conscious You never makes a severe mis-take, and it can learn from all of its decisions and use them as a springboard for growth. The Conscious You simply learns from its mistakes without feeling guilty and without condemn-ing itself.

What is difficult for most people to understand is that the true purpose of the Conscious You's descent is not the building of the castle. The process of building the castle is just a tool to facilitate the Conscious You's growth in self-awareness. As the Conscious You exercises its free will and multiplies its talents, it gradually grows in wisdom and awareness. It can expand the crystalline structure of the soul vehicle (the four lower bodies) and it can magnify the light contained in that structure. The ultimate goal is that the Conscious You eventually attains such a strong self-awareness that it accepts that it is a self-sufficient being that is independent of anything in this world.

In the beginning, the Conscious You can exist only because it receives a stream of spiritual energy from the I AM Presence and it sees the Presence as being separated from itself. This light streams through the open door of the threefold flame. As the Conscious You grows so does its threefold flame, and the Conscious You can now transmit more light. As the Conscious You's self-awareness grows, it begins to achieve the Christ consciousness, which makes the Conscious You realize that it is not simply an extension of the Presence. The Conscious You is not actually a separate being that exists apart from the

I AM Presence and is merely connected to that Presence. The Conscious You realizes that it is actually one with the I AM Presence, and the Conscious You now exclaims: "I and my Father are one!" (John 10:30).

The Conscious You has now attained Christ conscious-ness and can walk the earth as a Christed being who can bring God's kingdom to earth. However, the Conscious You can build upon this and achieve a higher level of self-awareness. The next step is that the Conscious You realizes that its I AM Presence is part of a larger whole, a hierarchy of spiritual beings that reaches all the way to the highest manifestation of God. The light that the Conscious You receives from the I AM Presence is actually the light of God that streams through the Presence and into the threefold flame. That light comes from the source, which is God.

The Conscious You realizes the truth in the statement that "without him was not anything made that was made" (John 1:3). Everything was made from God's light and his light is within everything. Everything has the potential to draw upon that light directly from within itself. The Conscious You now realizes that it no longer needs to receive God's light from a distant I AM Presence because it can receive that light directly from within itself. We might also say that the Conscious You realizes that the I AM Presence is not "up there" in a higher realm but that the I AM Presence is right here with the Con-scious You. There really is no distance or separation between the Conscious You and the Presence.

At that moment, the Conscious You is no longer a planet orbiting the sun of the I AM Presence. The Conscious You now becomes a sun in its own right; it becomes a self-lumi-nous being that radiates the light of God directly from within itself. At that moment, the Conscious You becomes a spiritual master and wins a permanent self-awareness. This does not mean that the Conscious You separates itself from the I AM Presence. It means that the Conscious You becomes one with the I AM Presence and through that oneness the Conscious You realizes that it is part of a larger whole, namely the Body of God.

This is the natural growth process of a lifestream, and many lifestreams did indeed follow this pattern before the Fall occurred. Every lifestream still has the potential to follow that pattern, but it has become more difficult because in order to achieve permanent self-awareness, a lifestream must give up the false self-awareness that springs from the human ego.

To explain the Fall and the birth of the human ego, let us start with the story of the Garden of Eden. Let me make it clear that this story does not apply to all lifestreams on earth and it should not be taken literally. It does contain truth, and it can also be used to expose some of the serpentine lies inserted into the Bible.

As explained earlier, the Garden was a mystery school in which lifestreams received education in the mechanics of the material universe as their preparation for taking on a material body. The God in the garden was a representative of God, a spiritual teacher by the name of Maitreya. He had designed a step-by-step process that would allow a Conscious You to take on a material body without losing its connection to the I AM Presence. Certain lifestreams became impatient with the graded lessons and decided to jump ahead. Some did this in an act of rebellion, others followed the leaders and still others simply let their curiosity get the better of them. The result was that a number of lifestreams (far more than two) began to slip into the dualistic state of consciousness.

At some point – individual for every lifestream – the Conscious You had a moment of truth, and it realized that it had lost its connection to the I AM Presence—it had fallen from grace. At that moment, the Conscious You had to make an all-important decision. Some lifestreams chose to go back to the teacher and take responsibility for their mistakes. These lifestreams were received with unconditional love and were given help to regain their spiritual connection. Unfortunately, some lifestreams decided that they did not want to face the teacher and take responsibility for their mistakes, and as a result they decided to hide from the teacher. Because of the Law of Free Will, the teacher could not go after these lifestreams. He had to stand back and respect their choice, allowing them to learn from their own experiences instead of from his experience. Only when a Conscious You asks for help, can the teacher help that student.

It is essential for spiritual seekers to realize that the biblical account is erroneous in several ways. In reality, the fallen lifestreams were not forcefully cast out of the Garden. They simply lowered their consciousness until they could no longer perceive the Garden, which still exists in a level of higher vibrations. God is not trying to keep lifestreams from returning to the Garden, but the false teachers are trying to do so. The main weapon these forces use in order to keep the Conscious You away from its spiritual teacher is the human ego so let us look at the birth of the ego.

At the moment of truth, the Conscious You realized that it had lost its connection to the I AM Presence. If the Conscious You went back to the teacher, it would gradually regain this connection and the self-awareness of being an extension of the spiritual self. If the Conscious You turned its back on the teacher, it would now have to build a new self-awareness based on the sense of being separated from its source. This new self-awareness is the human ego, and it springs from the sense of separation. The ego is not simply born of separation in a general sense. It reflects the reasoning that the Conscious

You used to justify its decision to turn away from the teacher. In order to give up the ego, the Conscious You must recognize and acknowledge the fallacy of this decision and replace it with a better decision. The Conscious You must consciously undo the decision that caused it to turn away from the teacher and the spiritual path. There are a number of reasons why lifestreams decided to turn away from the teacher, but let me mention just a few:

• Some lifestreams deliberately rebelled against the teacher, and their egos are based on the belief that God is wrong and that the lifestream knows better than God. These lifestreams often feel very capable and think they know everything. They can actually climb high on the spiritual path by following this momentum, yet in the end they face the supreme challenge of admitting that their egos do not know better than God and that they cannot enter Heaven by their own efforts.

• Some lifestreams followed other lifestreams who served as their leaders, and their egos are based on the concept that they should obey a higher authority and that they do not need to take responsibility for their lives and make their own decisions. Such lifestreams can make substantial spiritual progress by following a spiritual teacher. In the end they must abandon the tendency to follow outer leaders, take responsibility for their salvation and decide to follow only the authority of the Christ within them.

• Some lifestreams simply used their curiosity to experiment, and they often think they could never do anything really wrong and that everything will turn out okay in the end. These lifestreams can also make great spiritual progress, and they are often very open to the spiritual path. In the end they must overcome the belief that "anything goes" and acknowledge that all of their choices have consequences and that some consequences take them away from oneness with the I AM Presence. You can exercise your curiosity safely only by using Christ discernment. These lifestreams must surrender their curiosity and desire for freedom to the higher authority of the Christ within them.

The birth of the human ego is tied to certain negative emotions. Some lifestreams fear God, some become angry, some become prideful, some feel they are unworthy or unacceptable in the eyes of God and some want to hide from God. Many lifestreams have a combination of such emotions that they must work through before they can make peace with God.

When you step back from the many reasons why lifestreams turned away from the teacher, you see that an important element of the ego is the sense of separation from the I AM Presence. As I said, the Conscious You was never meant to be alone so this separation gives the Conscious You a deep sense of insecurity.

As long as the Conscious You is in contact with its spiritual teacher, it does not feel insecure because it knows the teacher will always be there. When it loses that connection, the insecurity appears and it becomes a dominant part of the lifestream's self-awareness. For some lifestreams the insecurity becomes an unbearable trauma that they simply cannot live with. To overcome the sense of insecurity, the ego now steps in and attempts to take over the role of the spiritual teacher and I AM Presence. The ego seeks to give the Conscious You a sense of security, but because the ego is born of separation and is made from the lower vibrations of the duality consciousness, the ego can never make the Conscious You feel fully secure. The ego is attempting to create a false sense of security that is based on the sand of the material world. Because this world is ever-changing, the Conscious You can never feel completely secure in this world. While this is painful for the Conscious You, it is also a lifeline to the spiritual realm because the lifestream cannot be completely lost in duality.

In its attempt to provide the Conscious You security, the ego attempts to control the person's outer circumstances and its world view. For example, rebellious lifestreams will build a mental image that God is wrong and that they know best. They will often seek positions of power in society, and they will seek to control all other people in order to maintain the illusion that they are right. They will set themselves up as idols. This appeals to the lifestreams who fell because they did not make their own decisions. These lifestreams are looking for idols in order to maintain the illusion that they can be saved by following a strong leader. The lifestreams who fell because of curiosity don't want to accept any restrictions of their experimentation. They build the illusion that nothing is really wrong and that by experimenting with, and perfecting, the dualistic state of consciousness they will eventually get back to the Garden.

The common denominator is that the human ego is based on an illusion, a lie, and that it will always seek to control the Conscious You, other people and the universe in its attempt to maintain this illusion. The ego will actively and aggressively prevent the Conscious You from seeing through the illusion that created the ego. Once the ego is created, it attains a certain sense of self-awareness, and with that comes a survival instinct. The ego knows that if the Conscious You abandons the illusion that created the ego, the ego will die. In order to stay alive, the ego has to keep the Conscious You trapped in illusion.

Some spiritual teachers say we can perfect or raise up the ego, but that isn't correct, is it?

It is not. The ego was born out of the Conscious You's sense of separation from its spiritual source. The only way – and I mean the absolutely only way – that the Conscious You can be saved is to overcome that sense of separation and attain a sense of oneness with its I AM Presence. For that to happen, the ego simply must die. The Conscious You must come to see through the illusion that gave birth to the ego, and the Conscious You must then decide to leave that illusion behind for good. That act will become the acceptable offering, the acceptable sacrifice, that will realign the Conscious You with its source.

The ego will never let go of the illusion that created it, and consequently there is no way to perfect the ego. The Conscious You must leave the ego behind and allow it to die. As I said, you cannot serve two masters, God or mammon (Matthew 6:24). Mammon is another word for the ego, and in order to be saved, you must choose whom you will serve (Joshua 24:15). You must choose life (Deuteronomy 30:19), the life of your I AM Presence.

The dream of perfecting the ego springs from pride. It is created by lifestreams who will not admit that they made a mistake so they want to make it seem like they were not wrong for falling into a lower state of consciousness. They will not admit that the ego is unreal, and they are trying to perfect it so they can eventually go back to the teacher and show their perfect creation. They think this will work, but it is an illusion that is doomed from the beginning. It is another example of the way that seems right unto a human, but it can never lead you to Heaven.

How do we overcome the ego?

As I have explained in the previous book, you must learn how to let go, how to surrender your limited beliefs and your limited sense of identity. Letting go and surrendering is an essential part of the spiritual path, and unfortunately many spiritual seekers have not understood this point.

The problem here is that before the Conscious You fell, it knew that it could not act on its own. It knew that it could act only by using the light of God, and it realized that it could receive that light only from the I AM Presence. After the Conscious You fell, it began to see itself as separated from the I AM Presence and it eventually forgot that the Presence exists. It was inevitable that the Conscious You now began to think that it could act on its own. After a lifestream falls, it is still receiving the light from its I AM Presence, even though it is not consciously aware of this. If a lifestream misuses this light, it can eventually be cut off from the I AM Presence so that it is not receiving any light. At that point, a lifestream can continue to exist only by stealing light from other people. Of course, doing so only cements the lifestream's sense that it can act on its own.

As I explained earlier, when a lifestream discovers the path, it is still influenced by the illusion that it is acting on its own. It therefore engages in the path with the thought that it can walk the path by its own efforts. In one sense this is true, because, as I explained when I talked about the outer path, certain elements of the path are somewhat mechanical. You can actually make some progress through your own efforts, however you are still using the light of God to produce that progress.

As the lifestream climbs the path, it eventually hits a level from which it can make no further progress until it begins to understand the need to surrender its imperfect beliefs and sense of identity. Many lifestreams have become stuck at that level for lifetimes. The key to moving higher is to realize that you have to let go of your illusions instead of seeking to justify them. When you can understand this one point, you graduate to a much higher level of the path. You now begin to realize that the entire idea that you are the doer is an illusion. In reality, you are not separated from your I AM Presence and everything you do is done with God's light.

You now realize that you cannot do your way back to Heaven. You cannot be saved by continuing to do with the dualistic mind. The key is to surrender, to let go of, all dualistic beliefs until you reclaim your connection to, and eventually attain oneness with, your I AM Presence. It is surrendering, rather than doing that is the real key to spiritual progress.

To fully surrender, you must overcome the human ego's need to control everything. You must surrender the will of the ego – which most lifestreams have come to see as their own will – to the will of a higher authority, namely a spiritual teacher and your Christ self. This can be very difficult for some lifestreams because they have come to identify themselves fully with the ego. They truly think that the ego, and its insatiable desire for control, is a necessary and beneficial part of their identity that they cannot – and should not – live without. The only solution is that the lifestream follows the spiritual path and learns to surrender its illusions. By building a momentum on surrender and the sacrifice of illusions, the Conscious You will eventually build the inner strength that empowers it to tackle the final illusion of the ego. If the Conscious You truly bonds with its Christ self and spiritual teacher, it will not be all that difficult to overcome the ego. You will naturally come to a point where you realize that nothing in this world is worth holding on to if it prevents you from attaining Christ consciousness. You are willing to lose your mortal life in order to win the eternal life of the Christ consciousness (Matthew 16:25).

> **I have thought a lot about the difference between being and doing. I have noticed that many people are preoccupied with doing things instead of simply being. How can we overcome this tendency to take Heaven by force—by doing instead of being?**

The difference between being and doing is the essential challenge of human existence. The difference between being and doing is the difference between the Christ consciousness and the dualistic consciousness.

I cannot give you an intellectual understanding of the difference between doing and being because the intellect cannot fathom being. When the Conscious You loses contact with the spiritual realm, it begins to reason with the intellect, and its actions are heavily influenced by the emotions. Both of these faculties are relative faculties. This does not mean that there is something inherently wrong with the intellect or the emotions. These faculties are designed to help the Conscious You express itself in the material world. They are meant to be the servants of the Conscious You, and the Conscious You must take command over them. To do this, the Conscious You must have a guiding rod that is above and beyond the relativity of the intellect and the emotions. This can happen only through the lifestream's contact with the Christ self. When the Conscious You loses that contact, it no longer has a guiding rod for keeping the intellect and emotions in line with the laws of God. The Conscious You easily becomes overwhelmed by the relativity of intellect and emotions. Instead of being the servant of the Conscious You, the intellect and the emotions tend to take over and enslave the Conscious You. The human ego will use the intellect and the emotions to control the Conscious You, and unless the Conscious You stands on the rock of Christ, it has little defense against this attack.

When the Conscious You is using the lower mind as the basis for its actions, the person is in a mode of being the doer. The Conscious You sees itself as the doer because it has lost its connection to the spiritual realm. This becomes one of the major stumbling blocks for people on the spiritual path. Many people on earth are completely absorbed in the lower consciousness, and they have no concept of a spiritual path. When the Conscious You awakens from this sleep and begins to realize that there is a path, the person inevitably looks at the path through the filter of the lower mind. Before the Conscious You was awakened to the spiritual side of life, it was completely absorbed in doing with the outer mind. When the Conscious You recognizes the spiritual path, it usually thinks that the way to walk the path is to keep doing with the outer mind.

Before a Conscious You is awakened, it is doing with the outer mind. Now the Conscious You is awakened and realizes that its former actions sabotaged its progress on the path. It is very easy to reason that it was specific outer actions that presented a problem. If you abstain from those actions and engage in actions that are seen as more spiritual, you must be moving forward on the spiritual path. This is both true and untrue.

When you are trapped in the relativity of the lower mind, you can justify anything. Certain people feel justified in committing selfish acts that violate the rights of other people. When you commit such acts, you misqualify God's energy, and this karma forms an obstacle to your spiritual progress.

If you reform your actions and do more unselfish acts, you will increase your progress on the spiritual path. However, the true goal of the spiritual path is to bring you closer to God. This closeness is more than anything a state of consciousness, a sense of identity, an inner feeling of being one with God. That state of mind cannot be produced by doing; it can only come about by being.

When people are first awakened to the spiritual path, they are still so affected by the lower consciousness that they think they have to do their way back to Heaven. They think walking the path is a matter of performing outer actions, and they determine those actions by using the relativity of the death consciousness. That is why you see many people who begin the spiritual path by being very intellectual or very emotional. They are following the outer path that we talked about earlier.

You can find people who see themselves as being highly spiritual, yet they spend most of their time intellectualizing about this or that aspect of the spiritual path without ever developing a true inner understanding of the path. We might say that they know a lot, but have internalized very little. You can find other people who are driven by strong emotions. Such people often cling to the belief that one particular idea or doctrine is infallible and they become fanatical in defending their beliefs or following outer rules. These people have a strong drive to move forward, but it is aimed in the wrong direction.

I am not saying this to criticize anyone. When you first awaken to the spiritual path, it is natural and inevitable that your approach to the path is affected by the death consciousness. You will go through an interim period in which you seek to do your way back to Heaven. What I would like people to understand is that by being consciously aware of how the ego influences your approach to the spiritual path, you can greatly shorten this interim period. Even more importantly, you can avoid being stuck in a blind alley, which happens to many people.

If you observe people in spiritual movements, you will see that many of them went through a period in which they were openly searching for a higher spiritual truth. At some point, they found a particular organization or doctrine, and they began to believe that this was what they had been looking for. After having found that organization, they closed their minds to ideas that came from any other source—including their Christ selves. People often use a particular organization or doctrine as an excuse for closing their minds. People have stopped searching, yet they believe that because they belong to a particular organization, they are highly spiritual and they are making maximum progress on the path.

As I have said before, the essence of the path is that you are constantly moving toward a higher awareness of the spiritual side of life. No outer organization or doctrine can capture a complete understanding of the mysteries of God. If you want to make maximum progress on the spiritual path, you cannot confine your search to one particular doctrine or organization. You cannot afford to stop searching. You must constantly be searching for a higher experience of God, and you must be willing to look for understanding wherever it can be found. If you confine your search to one particular doctrine or belief system, you are no longer making maximum progress on the path. You might be making progress, but you are not making progress as rapidly as you could by remaining open to the truly transforming directions that can only come from your Christ self instead of an outer source.

To get back to my original point, the essence of the spiritual path is that you rise above the death consciousness, the consciousness in which you are doing with the lower mind. The essential key to making maximum progress is that you become consciously aware of how the lower mind influences your approach to life. You must begin to see the difference between doing with the lower mind and simply being. At first, this might seem difficult. However, any person walking the spiritual path has experienced the difference between doing and being. Consider how you handle situations in which you have to make an important decision. In some cases, you are using the intellect to argue back and forth without coming up with a final answer. Every option you can imagine seems to have certain drawbacks, and you cannot decide which one is the lesser evil. At other times, you might be very emotional, coming from a state of fear that if you do the wrong thing, undesirable consequences will be the result. In both cases, you are clearly acting from the lower mind and that is why you do not have inner peace.

Everyone has experienced an entirely different approach to difficult situations. Sometimes you have an intuitive insight and you know what is the right course of action. In such cases, your intellect is pushed in the background because you have no need to reason back and forth. Your emotions are neutralized because you have no fear or doubts about the outcome. You simply know what to do, and you feel a sense of inner peace about it. The sense of knowing and being at peace comes from your Christ self.

When you lose the connection to your Christ self, you have only the relativity of the death consciousness, and that is why you are like a wave of the sea that is driven by the wind and tossed (James 1:6). When you are connected to your Christ self, you have the inner peace that comes from standing on the rock of Christ. When you are influenced by the intellect and emotions, you are doing. When you are influenced by the Christ self, you are being.

Every person on the spiritual path has experienced an intuitive connection to his or her Christ self. If you did not have this connection, you would not be on the spiritual path. It really is that simple. To resolve the difference between doing and being, you need to focus your attention on expanding your connection to your Christ self. As you expand that connection, you will move away from doing and gradually move into being. To speed up the process, use the tools I have mentioned in these books and on our website [*www.transcendencetoolbox. com*].

12 | TO DISCERN OR NOT TO DISCERN

You have talked about the need to develop what you call Christ discernment. I know many people are bewildered by this and I can understand why. When we are blinded by the death consciousness we simply have no frame of reference for even grasping what Christ discernment is. I have met many people who are so afraid of being wrong or afraid of dark forces that they don't dare to practice discernment. How do you suggest people can get started?

For those who want to go beyond what is given in these books, I suggest they follow my *Course in Christhood*. It is designed precisely for that purpose. The teachings, the exercises, together form the best way that is currently available to increase your discernment.

There is no magical formula—there is no magical key that I can give you that will instantly give you discernment. It is truly a matter of practice makes perfect. In order to start practicing discernment, you have to be willing to be wrong. If you are not willing to be wrong, you cannot learn how to be right.

You must be willing to use whatever ability you have now to experiment and then learn from those experiments—without condemning yourself when you make a mistake. So many people, so many spiritual students, are actually afraid to practice discernment. They are so afraid of tuning in to any lower energies that they dare not use their discernment. But how can you learn to walk unless you practice? No one – no baby on earth – has ever gotten up and walked on the first try. No one has ever developed discernment in one instant—it cannot happen.

Some spiritual students have become so afraid of being influenced by psychic forces or by the false hierarchy that they do not dare to practice their discernment. They confine themselves to a particular mental box that they cannot get out of until at some point in the future they decide to T-R-Y try. TRY stands for Theos Rules You and no one can make progress on the spiritual path without making an effort beyond what you have done so far. Why have they not tried? It can be only fear, and as long as you are in fear you cannot actually have discernment.

If you are so afraid of making a mistake that you are more afraid of being mistaken than you have a love for being right, then you are in a catch-22. The only way to break that catch-22 is to use your will, your conscious will, to decide that you are willing to try. Even if you make a mistake, you will learn from it and go from there, and you will ask the ascended masters – in whatever way you conceive of us – to help you with that discernment—and we will.

But you must be willing to multiply the talents. For those who are not multiplying the talents, well then, we are not allowed to help you. We must leave you where you are, until you decide to raise your consciousness by experimenting, by being co-creators.

What does it mean to be a co-creator? It means to experiment. Creativity cannot be predefined. It is spontaneous, and it is only those who are trapped in fear who want a guarantee ahead of time, the guarantee that if they get up and try to walk, they will not fall down. No baby has ever gotten that guarantee—and no spiritual student will ever get a guarantee that if they try to develop discernment, they will not make mistakes.

You do indeed see those who are potentially good students of the ascended masters, but they have been trapped in this catch-22 of not daring to exercise their discernment. They do not even dare to look at a new teaching, for they have already decided that it must be psychic or it must be the false hierarchy.

But you cannot discern that with the analytical mind—you can discern that only with the heart. But the heart needs to be applied, and you cannot apply it if you are not willing to take a look. It is like the situation from the movie *Chariots of Fire* where the runner says to his girlfriend: "If I can't win, I won't run." She answers back: "If you won't run, you can't win."

The ego and the dualistic mind will obviously interfere with our discernment so how do we get beyond that?

There are many tools that can help you do this, and some are described on our toolbox website, *www.transcendencetoolbox.com*. I have also mentioned the *Course in Christhood*. Let me mention a few tools that are not described elsewhere.

It can be very helpful for you to begin by adopting a certain world view, a certain approach to life. As part of this approach, I encourage you to acknowledge the simple fact that as long as you are in this material universe, you will always have remnants of the ego or the dualistic mind. You should let go of the immature idea that there is some automatic or final solution whereby you will be permanently free of the need to discern between reality and unreality. As long as this universe is in an imperfect state, you will need to exercise discernment even after you attain a high degree of Christhood.

It will also be helpful to a acknowledge the fact that in the material universe there is no such thing as an absolute or final expression of truth. Give up the idea that you need to find an absolute or unquestionable belief system or doctrine. Instead, acknowledge the fact that you are following a path whereby you will gain successively deeper insights into the true nature of life and God. I can assure you that while you are in this universe, you can always find a deeper understanding of truth. I can give you this assurance because even I do to not claim to have attained the full understanding of God and of God's truth.

Many people have the image that they are lost and that they need to find some outer thing that will save them. Once they have found that outer thing, which they often see as a particular belief system or religion, they think their search is over. What I am encouraging you to realize is that growth is ongoing, and it will never come to a halt in this universe.

Always continue to seek for a deeper understanding than what you currently have. Do not seek the ultimate or absolute understanding. Seek the understanding that will help you take the next step on your personal path. After you take that step, you will be ready to attain an even higher understanding.

After you adopt this new approach to life, make a sincere effort to put on personal Christhood. I understand that this process can seem overwhelming or confusing in the beginning. I suggest that you use a particular belief system as the foundation for your search.

For example, if you are currently a Christian, use the Christian scriptures as your lodestone or guiding rod. However, instead of seeing the scriptures as absolute and instead of holding on to a literal or fundamentalist interpretation of the scriptures, allow your higher self to give you a deeper understanding of the meaning of the scriptures.

I am not suggesting that you throw yourself into an identity crisis and throw away everything that you have so far believed in. I am suggesting that you open your mind to a deeper understanding of your current belief system and then use that as a foundation for your continued, never-ending growth in understanding.

As you keep growing in understanding, be aware that you might benefit from studying spiritual teachings that are not part of your current belief system. If you feel an inner prompting to do so, dare to follow that prompting and do not close your mind to this inner direction. For example, you might acknowledge that throughout the centuries there have been a number of Christian mystics. Dare to study some of their writings.

Be aware that the primary weapon of the dualistic mind is to somehow, often through fear and doubt, make you cling to your current beliefs. It is the dualistic mind that wants to keep you in a mental prison where there is no growth. Your higher mind and your spiritual teachers, including myself, always want you to move on to a deeper understanding of life.

It is all a matter of which way you decide to follow. Will you follow the way that seems right onto a human, the way of attachment, fear and a closed mind. The way that causes people to think that the road to salvation goes through an outer organization or doctrine. Or will you follow the true way, the way of an ever increasing understanding through personal Christhood.

It seems to me that Christ discernment is a very fine balance, almost like the fine balance between people who are creative geniuses but often become unbalanced and become almost mad. How can we find the best balance on the spiritual path?

Let us define creativity. In any given society, there is a mass consciousness that overpowers the minds of most people and causes them to think within certain boundaries, what I call a mental box. Creativity can be defined as the ability and willingness to open your mind to something that is outside the mental box of your society. You can then bring forth ideas that people overpowered by the collective consciousness could not have received.

Of course, in many cases people limited by the mental box may not see a new idea as a stroke of genius. Most people will cling to their mental box and will reject anything that is too far beyond the box. As a society evolves, the mental box can be expanded, and more and more people will then begin to accept ideas that were previously rejected. This was the case with the fact that the earth is not the center of the universe and many other ideas.

I mention this because one of the factors contributing to "creative insanity" is that creative people often feel rejected or misunderstood. I might say, based on my own experience, that as long as they don't nail you to a wooden cross, you really shouldn't complain too much. However, it is constructive to see your own efforts as part of the larger stream – the River of Life – that brings humanity forward. If you can take this longer view, you will not feel rejected because you will know that a new idea is rarely embraced in the beginning. You can avoid some of the feeling of rejection—depending on the strength of your desire for recognition, as I will talk about later.

Of course, it would be naive to say that any idea which is beyond the mental box of a given society is necessarily a creative or ingenious idea. There are ideas which are not creative in the sense that they do not contribute to the forward progression of humanity. Such ideas may be destructive or they may be variations of existing ideas that do not help people or society grow.

On the one hand, a creative genius can be defined as a person whose mind is open to something beyond the collective mental box of his or her society. When we realize that not every idea is constructive, we need to add a distinction. We need to ask: "When a person is open to something beyond the collective mental box, what exactly is it to which the person is open?"

Here, of course, is where neither mainstream Christianity nor materialistic science can give a satisfactory answer. The key insight missing from both thought systems is the fact that there are several levels of the material universe, namely the physical, the emotional, the mental and the etheric.

Especially on the emotional and mental levels, you find many beings who have become trapped there for a time. These beings will often seek to work with human beings, especially those who are more sensitive than the average person. The disembodied beings will promise people certain benefits, and one of them can be the ability to bring forth ideas that are distinctly outside the mental box of society.

For example, many modern musicians work with beings in the emotional realm to bring forth music that is new and different. At the same time, we of the ascended masters also seek to work with sensitive individuals to bring forth new forms of music. What is the difference? The difference is that an ascended being needs nothing from you whereas the unascended beings in lower realms do need something from you, namely your psychic energy. An ascended being will not descend below a certain level so we will only work with people who are able to raise their consciousness and tune in to our higher vibrations. All people have the ability to tune in to vibrations beyond the collective mental box, but the question is to which degree it is developed:

- The average person has not developed these so-called psychic abilities, and he or she rarely receives any impulse from beyond the collective mental box.

- Some people have developed their psychic abilities, but they have not developed much discrimination. They are open to anything beyond the collective mental box and do not discern as to whether it is from the ascended masters or a lower source.

- A few people have developed their psychic abilities to have various degrees of discernment. Some can tell whether an impulse is emotionally unbalanced, but they can still be fooled by something from the mental realm. Others can tell the difference in vibration between the mental realm and the ascended realm.

You now begin to see the distinction that must be made. People who are sensitive can receive impulses from a realm beyond the collective mental box. What they receive will depend on their ability to attune their consciousness to certain vibrations. That in turn depends on the contents of their minds and personal energy fields.

If people have a lot of disharmonious emotional energy accumulated in their energy fields, they cannot tune in to anything higher than the emotional level. Beings in the emotional level are eager to work with sensitive people, and they can give you a certain empowerment. For example, you see certain musicians who have a strong stage presence that can get an audience to go into a frantic state of mind. The reason for this is that the person allows a spirit in the emotional realm to possess him or her. This being can be strong enough to overpower the audience at a concert and whip their emotions into a highly unbalanced state. This causes them to release light from their chakras, which the spirit in the emotional realm can then absorb and use to survive or expand its powers. [For more detailed teachings on such spirits, see *Flowing With the River of Life*.]

What the person who is open to the emotional spirit gets in return is the empowerment that can make that person famous because the person can do something that most people would never be able to do. The price that such a person has to pay is that his or her emotions are magnified to a point where the person simply cannot maintain a normal balance and harmony, which is what can lead to various episodes that can indeed resemble madness. This extreme imbalance also often makes a person highly susceptible to drug abuse, as a way to mechanically recreate the altered state of consciousness experienced when the person is possessed by an emotional spirit.

The unbalanced emotions are especially problematic when coupled with a strong desire for recognition. Getting public attention can very quickly become an addiction. The person craving it will then go into more and more extreme behavior in order to get the one thing to which the person is addicted: attention of any kind. There is a saying that bad publicity is better than no publicity, and for some people the same holds true for attention. They will do almost anything to get it, and they can become highly imbalanced if they do not get enough of it. The problem with an addiction being that you can never get enough of what you crave. Another case is spirits in the mental realm, and they do not work with people's emotions. Instead, they can overpower certain people to set themselves up as teachers in various areas of society, including as spiritual teachers. Some of these spirits do have a sophisticated intellectual understanding of many concepts. They can easily empower a person so he or she can impress the average intellects. What you might learn to sense from spirits in the mental realm is that they are often quite unclear and give teachings that are highly complex. This is done in order to overpower the intellect of the average person so that people surrender their critical thinking to the teacher and to the spirit overpowering the teacher. Again, this is done to steal people's psychic energy.

People who are working with beings in the mental realm can often talk and talk, but it is difficult to figure out exactly what they are saying. They often hint at advanced teachings and use obscure language that few people understand—thus giving the impression that if you don't understand, it is because you are not as advanced as they are. Another characteristic is that such people only talk and rarely or never take action. The spirits working through them actually have as their goal to pacify you by having you think about spiritual matters without doing anything to transcend the mental box they have created for you. They want to make you think you are getting advanced teachings and keep you engaged indefinitely.

It is one of the facts of life on this planet that many well-meaning people have become trapped in this intellectual blind alley, thinking they understand but failing to realize that real change cannot come from the mental level alone. Only when you take your ideas into the emotional and physical realms, will there be change. Universities and spiritual movements are full of people who think they can think their way to a better world and who can spend an entire lifetime thinking, without locking in to the River of Life that would allow them to flow beyond the mental level.

In contrast, we of the ascended masters are not seeking to appear clever or sophisticated. We are instead seeking to present our teachings in a way that is clear and easy to understand. We are not coming from a need to impress but a desire to awaken. Furthermore, we always encourage action, such as giving invocations, questioning your mental box and engaging in society.

What you now see is that there are many people who have a sensitivity that is beyond the average. If they have not purified their energy fields and have not developed discernment, they are likely to open themselves up to spirits in the mental and emotional realms or even the lower identity realm. Such spirits will always want something in return, namely your energy, which they get over your attention and by engaging you, either in endless intellectual musings or inharmonious emotional patterns.

One might indeed say that the collective mental box is both a blessing and a curse. It is a limitation in that it prevents people and societies from embracing constructive ideas. It is a blessing in that it serves as a kind of protection that prevents many people from opening themselves up to lower forces and non-constructive ideas.

This is not to say that I am hereby encouraging people to cling to the collective mental box. I am indeed encouraging anyone with sensitivity to pay attention to the need to develop discernment and to practice spiritual techniques in order to protect one's energy field from lower forces and to purify it from lower energies.

On our toolbox website, we give various techniques for spiritual protection and for the purification of the energy field, and this is a good place to start. By studying various spiritual teachings and seeking to develop intuition, one can then gradually build discernment. However, this must begin with the recognition that it is necessary to discern between higher and lower "creative" impulses. This realization must be followed up by a decision that you want this discernment and that you are willing to work for it.

One might say that there truly is not a fine line between genius and madness. True genius is the ability to tune in to the ascended realm. Attuning to anything below that is a form of madness, and it is only a question of how unbalanced the person ends up becoming.

That question is largely determined by the person's willingness to learn. You will see many people who are open to something beyond the collective mental box but who are driven by a personal ambition combined with pride. They have a clear ambition of being recognized as being unusual or even superior. This often causes them to be very closed-minded to the possibility that they could tune in to lower forces or that they need to work on discernment. They think that any idea or force that makes them stand out from the crowd must be good, and they are reluctant to give it up.

This explains why many of the geniuses that have been recognized throughout history have ended up their days in a severely imbalanced state of mind. Many of them were able to occasionally tune in to the ascended realm and receive one or several ideas that brought society forward. They were later undone by their lack of balance in the emotional body or by the intellectual pride that prevented them from consciously working on discernment.

You cannot develop discernment if you have the attitude that you can never be wrong. You develop any ability only by practicing, and that means you will be wrong many times, but when you learn from this, it can be turned into stepping stones to progress.

The clear recognition that we of the ascended masters have is that for the golden age to become a reality, millions of people must develop their mind's abilities so they can become open doors for new ideas. We are dedicated to giving people the teachings and the tools to accomplish this. It is highly appropriate to encourage people to use caution. Be willing to take an honest look at yourself:

• Do you find that your feelings are often drawn into inharmonious or unbalanced reactions? Then, go to work on protecting and purifying your energy field.

• Do you find that you have a tendency to think you should always be right and can never have been wrong? Then consider the need to overcome pride by being willing to learn from both your higher self and other people.

• Do you find that you have a desire for recognition? If so, be willing to seek first the kingdom of God, namely a connection to your I AM Presence. For when you have that, you will know that you need no recognition from this world.

• Above all, realize that the foremost key to becoming the open door that no man can shut is to attain balance in all things. Some people think it is necessary to take an extreme stand in order to combat dark forces or demonstrate higher principles to society. Taking a stand can very well be done without being in an unbalanced frame of mind.

The brutal fact is that too many people have been the open door for a few ideas. But then their own imbalances have shut the door and their full potential never came to fruition. Becoming the open door that no man can shut has two sides. One is that you do not let dark forces or the mass consciousness prevent you from expressing new ideas. But the other is that you do not allow your own personal imbalances to take you into extremes where you are no longer the open door. Instead, you have shut the door through your pride, ambition, emotional attachments or other imbalanced conditions in your mind.

The challenge I put before you is that being a creative genius requires you to be open to ideas beyond the collective mental box while at the same time being extremely balanced. If you think this sounds contradictory, then I submit that this proves you are in a state of imbalance. If you will use the tools we give on our toolbox website and make it your overall goal to find balance, then you will one day come to a point where the contradiction melts away. You now see that being open to the ascended realm does indeed require balance, namely the balance that only comes from complete non-attachment. I can of my own self do nothing; it is the I AM Presence within me who is doing the works.

You will see the truth of this only when you recognize that "you" are not the ego and the separate self, which wants recognition. "You" are the Conscious You, a clear pane of glass that has no ambition other than to be an open door for the Presence. Only by being in that state of balance and non-attachment, can you be an open door that does not color what comes from the Presence or seeks to use it for what the separate self perceives as personal gain.

I am not trying to make this sound extraordinarily difficult. What one has done; all can do. Many have already attained a high degree of balance that allows them to be the open door for golden age ideas. Many more could quickly become open doors by paying attention to the need to seek balance in all things.

Seek and ye shall find. The problem is that many creative people are not seeking balance. They are actually seeking to become more extreme so they can receive what they think are even more creative ideas—that will finally get them the recognition they crave. That is exactly what brings them to the edge of madness or beyond. ⓧ

13 | TAKE COMMAND OF YOUR IDENTITY

What do you consider to be the greatest challenge we encounter on the spiritual path?

The greatest challenge is to be who you are regardless of who the world wants you to be. You must express your God-given individuality, even when that individuality does not fit into the mold created by the world, by the people closest to you or by your human ego.

You live in a world that is heavily influenced by the dualistic state of consciousness. Dark forces and certain people have embodied that consciousness to such a degree that they do not want anyone to know that there is an alternative to duality. The forces of this world do not want you to embody your personal Christhood and express your God-given individuality because, by doing so, you demonstrate that there is indeed an alternative to the death consciousness.

The dark forces are attempting to gain complete control over planet earth. Because everything is subject to free will, these forces can only gain this control by manipulating human beings into making wrong choices. Currently, such forces have the upper hand because most people are so enveloped in the duality of the death consciousness that they are easy to manipulate. These forces want to keep humanity trapped in duality. They do not want to see the appearance of a person who has manifested Christ consciousness and is expressing his or her God-given individuality. Everything such a person does or says contradicts the lie that there is nothing beyond the death consciousness.

The dark forces, in cooperation with certain people on this planet, are attempting to control the general population by making people believe a multitude of false ideas, including the idea that there is no God or that the authority of God has been replaced by an earthly authority, such as the state or a church. As long as the formless God is seen as the ultimate authority, such people cannot gain ultimate power over the population. Once again, when you attain personal Christhood you become a threat to this power elite because you will not accept any earthly authority as being between you and God.

As you walk the spiritual path and attain Christhood, you should expect to become the target of dark forces. These forces will attack you by seeking to project certain thoughts and beliefs into your mind, especially false ideas relating to God, your relationship to God and your own self-worth. They will attempt to destroy your sense of self-worth and make you feel that you have no right to be who you are, to follow the spiritual path or to express your Christhood. To understand how such forces operate, read *The Screwtape Letters* by C. S. Lewis or study the story of my life.

These forces will also attack you by directing toxic energy at you in order to burden you with that energy. I am not saying this to frighten anyone or to make you concerned about walking the path. I am saying it because by being forewarned, you can be forearmed. I continually see people who start walking the spiritual path but are overwhelmed by the opposition from dark forces. The obvious reason is that people have been brought up with beliefs that either deny the existence of such forces or fail to provide a viable defense against these forces.

When it comes to opposition from other people, the best way to overcome it is to develop a clear and uncompromising respect for free will. You must realize that every human being has the right to react as he or she chooses. Do not become attached to other people's reactions to you or your spiritual path. It is extremely important, and I mean extremely important, that you do not engage in any kind of conflict or battle with other people. Do not allow them to drag you into dualistic conflicts, and do not feel like you have to convert them.

You must also maintain an uncompromising respect for your own free will. Even if the entire world is against you, you have a right to express your personal Christhood. You will see this demonstrated in my life. In the days before my crucifixion, almost everyone around me tried to talk me out of fulfilling my mission. For various reasons, they wanted me to change my ways and abstain from fulfilling what I knew was my mission and my destiny. I knew that they were simply reacting according to their level of spiritual maturity – or immaturity – and I remained non-attached.

I am not saying that you should ignore sound advice from others or use my words as an excuse for extremism. Some people have perverted the idea of being who you are, and they think it is acceptable to act on the ego's desires without any restrictions. Obviously, this has nothing to do with Christhood and spiritual growth. Balance is always the key to walking the path. However, you should acknowledge that every person – including yourself – has a right to live according to his or her present level of consciousness.

Obviously, every human being has a different mission. For many people, expressing Christhood might not be a public ministry. I am not trying to say that everyone will encounter the exact same outer circumstances that I encountered. Everyone will encounter some opposition from the world. The opposition will be aimed at derailing your spiritual progress and preventing you from attaining Christhood or expressing your God-given individuality. When you know this opposition is coming, you can avoid being derailed or even disturbed by it.

Learn from my example of how I was tempted by the devil. I remained non-attached to the temptations and did not engage the devil. I simply rebuked him by expressing what I saw as the highest truth. Learn from the wonderful example set by my brother, Gautama Buddha. He too was attacked by the demons of this world and remained non-attached. To demonstrate his right to manifest a higher consciousness in this world, he touched the ground and exclaimed "Vajra!" You must do the same. You must claim your right to bring the light of the Christ consciousness into the dark caverns of the death consciousness.

The bottom line is that as long as you think you need the world's permission in order to be the Christ, you cannot be the Christ. You must be the Christ regardless of the opposition from the forces of this world. Dare to be who you are and be non-attached to the reactions of others. Do not expect that the world will reward you for being the Christ in embodiment. Know that your reward will be in Heaven (Matthew 5:12), and it will be a greater reward than human beings can even imagine.

You have said that as we walk the spiritual path, we move into a more intuitive state of consciousness. Is that part of building a new sense of identity?

As I have tried to explain, humankind is engaged in a process of gradually raising its state of consciousness. This involves returning to a true sense of identity. After people sink into the lower state of consciousness, their sense of identity is distorted. The key to building a correct sense of identity is to attain balance in all parts of your being. The key to attaining balance is to use your intuition.

I came to inaugurate a spiritual age in which people were meant to rise to a more rational state of consciousness. Over the past 2,000 years, people have developed a far greater understanding of nearly every aspect of life. What needs to happen in the coming age is that people build upon the rational understanding developed by science and rise to the next evolutionary level. The unfortunate effect of the split between science and religion and the development of materialistic science is that science has glorified the human intellect.

The challenge faced by people in the current age is to overcome the glorification and the deification of rational thought and the intellect. People need to realize that the goal of humankind's evolutionary process is to rise above the dualistic state of consciousness. The human ego cannot be perfected, and it should be left behind. Rational thought is a very important stepping stone on that path, but it cannot take you all the way. Rational thought is meant to give people an understanding of the laws of God, but it is best suited for understanding the material laws. In the coming age, people need to rise above rational thought by using it as a foundation for intuitive exploration whereby they can come to know the spiritual laws. Only by fusing rational thought and intuitive insight can people gain a complete understanding of reality.

One might say that in past ages people were overpowered by their emotions. The development of rational thought has helped humankind rise above the hostility, superstition, extremism and fanaticism of the emotions. Unfortunately, many modern people are now stuck in intellectual reasoning. To make further progress, people need to recognize the value of intuition which allows them to reach into the identity or memory body and discover who they really are. This identity is anchored in your I AM Presence.

After you uncover your true identity, you can build on that foundation instead of continuing to build on the human ego. If you create a sense of identity with the lower mind, it will be a house built on sand. If you are a spiritual seeker, you want your identity to be built on the rock of the Christ consciousness. If you want to change undesirable patterns of behavior, follow what I consider to be one of my most pivotal remarks: "Seek first the kingdom of God – meaning the Christ consciousness – and all else shall be added unto you" (Matthew 6:33). Seek first to find your true identity as a spiritual being, and your thoughts, feelings and actions will be expressions of that sense of identity.

> **You often say that you came to demonstrate the spiritual path that all of us can follow and that you want us to look at you as an example. How many people can see your life as an example? I mean, take the Easter story. It is very difficult for us to identify with your crucifixion and all of the dramatic events surrounding it. Is there a message in your story that relates to our spiritual path?**

I understand your point so let me give you a different view of the Easter story. Let me first say that the Easter story is very rich and complex, and it can be interpreted in many different ways that can all be valid because each interpretation exposes a different facet of the story. However, I would like to present one perspective as food for thought. One of the main messages I seek to get across in these books is that I never desired to be elevated to an idol who was set apart from the rest of the people on this planet. I am not an egomaniac, as I am being portrayed by many Christians who insist on taking the biblical story literally or even embellishing upon it by making me into a god or a savior. I never wanted to be seen as so far above other people that they cannot possibly reach me or follow in my footsteps.

The message I would like all spiritual seekers to understand about the Easter story is that it is not about one person—it is not about me. In reality, it is the story of every lifestream, and it is meant to illustrate the path that every lifestream can follow. I realize that many Christians have been brought up with an idolized view of Jesus Christ, and they find it very difficult to free themselves from that idolatry. They insist that I was a unique person who is above and beyond anyone else ever to walk this planet.

I was indeed a unique person, and I did come on a unique spiritual mission. A very large part of that mission was to give forth a universal teaching relating to the spiritual potential for every lifestream on earth—because truly everyone is unique in the eyes of God. I not only gave that teaching through my spoken word; I demonstrated the teaching in my life. Every aspect of my life illustrates a part of the universal, inner teaching that I came to bring to this planet, and the Easter story is no exception. The Easter story is an illustration of the path that every lifestream can follow on its way to Christhood and its permanent ascension into the spiritual realm.

The Easter story can be broken down into three main elements. The first element is my entry into Jerusalem where I was welcomed by many people as a king. We might compare that to the birth of every child because most children are welcomed by their parents and family and treated as if they were someone special—which they are.

The second phase of the Easter story is what happened between my entry into Jerusalem and my resurrection. This phase illustrates what happens to the lifestream as it begins to grow up. You will note that the reason people welcomed me into Jerusalem was that they had a certain image of me. They had certain expectations of me being a king who would deliver them from the Romans, and they wanted me to live up to those expectations. However, it did not take long before many of them began to realize that I was not about to fulfill their expectations. Take note of how quick they were to turn on me when they realized I would not be bound by their expectations. Some of the same people who shouted hosannas at the gate were crying "Crucify him!" at my so-called trial. This is the story that the lifestream experiences as it grows up and begins to discover and express its individuality. The choice every lifestream faces is whether to conform to the expectations of the world, including parents, family and society, or whether to develop and express its unique individuality and fulfill its spiritual mission.

I am not hereby saying that every lifestream has the same spiritual maturity or spiritual mission. As I said when I described the levels of spiritual development, some lifestreams are not ready to complete the spiritual journey because they need healing or the resolution of their psychology. It is perfectly acceptable that some people live a life that is not particularly spiritual and that does not challenge the expectations of society. However, for the more mature lifestreams there will come a point where the Conscious You faces the choice of whether to deny its true individuality and spiritual mission in order to conform to the expectations of the world. My life was meant to illustrate that when you do reach that point of maturity, you need to be true to who you are. You need to fulfill your mission no matter what the world throws at you in response.   ⊗

My story was meant to inspire people with the courage to endure whatever persecution the world directs at them, and even go all the way and allow the world to kill their bodies, if the world decides to do so. Fortunately, we have now moved into a more civilized phase on this planet, and in many parts of the world you are not likely to be killed for expressing your spiritual individuality or pursuing your spiritual mission. Nevertheless, you are still likely to be exposed to a fair amount of persecution. Some of that persecution might come from people who consider themselves to be good Christians.

The important point in the Easter story is not the fact that I was killed. The important point is that I was willing to let the world kill me. Once again, this is described in my saying that he who seeks to save his life shall lose it, and he who is willing to lose his life for my sake shall find it (Matthew 16:25). The inner meaning is that if you submit to the expectations of the world and deny your spiritual identity, you will lose your life in a spiritual sense. If you remain true to your spiritual identity, even to the point of being willing to let the world kill your physical body, the Conscious You will find immortal life in the Christ consciousness.

The reality of the situation is that most people who dare to express their true identity and pursue their spiritual mission will be persecuted by the world. They might even be crucified in a spiritual sense, meaning that they will not be nailed to a physical cross but that they will be nailed to a spiritual cross by people's expectations. For example, many people have been spiritually crucified by the media in terms of a smear campaign or character assassination (of them personally or their spiritual beliefs or movement) that has portrayed them as falsely as I was portrayed by the temple priests.

The point is that if you are willing to allow the world to do whatever it wants to do with you, yet never for a moment deny your spiritual identity, you have the opportunity to go through the spiritual initiation of the resurrection. In my case, it was a physical resurrection to illustrate the potential for every lifestream to be resurrected into a higher state of consciousness and a higher sense of identity. This was meant to illustrate that the Conscious You can overcome the consciousness of death and win immortal life. What has not been understood by most Christians is that in order to win immortal life, the Conscious You must be willing to let its mortal sense of identity die on the cross.

The point being that even while I was hanging on the cross, I was facing the test of whether I would hold on to any part of my human sense of identity or whether I was willing to completely surrender that identity to God. Even though I momentarily felt abandoned by God, I did eventually surrender myself completely unto God. At that moment my physical body and my mortal sense of identity died, and at that moment I passed the spiritual initiation and won my resurrection.

I am not saying that every person has to go through the experience of being physically nailed to a cross and dying on that cross in order to be resurrected. Every Conscious You is crucified in a spiritual sense, meaning that it is hanging paralyzed on a cross made from its own karma, psychological wounds and imperfect beliefs. The Conscious You is nailed to that cross by the ego and the forces of this world. The Conscious You cannot take itself down from that cross—it can only surrender completely unto a higher power who will then raise the Conscious You above the cross and everything it represents.

Every lifestream must go through the experience of expressing its spiritual identity regardless of the persecution directed at it by the world. If the Conscious You remains true to its spiritual identity and is willing to give up every aspect of its human identity, then the Conscious You can win its resurrection. The resurrection means that the Conscious You has now transcended all human identity and has fully embraced a new identity as a son or daughter of God. The Conscious You has then passed the final exam on planet earth and has qualified for the ascension into the spiritual realm. The Conscious You is no longer bound by the wheel of rebirth and does not have to come back into embodiment on this planet. The Conscious You can permanently move into the spiritual realm and continue its journey from there.

It is my great hope that those who are spiritually ready, those who have ears to hear, will embrace this inner teaching about the Easter story so that in their minds and hearts they can experience a resurrection of my true inner teachings. The first thing that needs to happen to a spiritually aware person is that you are willing to be true to my inner teachings, no matter what kind of persecution you receive from the world, including from Christians who hold on to orthodox doctrines.

If you are willing to let go of all the man-made idols about me and my teachings, if you are willing to let those idols die, if you are willing to let the human sense of identity based on those idols die, then you can be resurrected into recognizing my true inner teachings. At that moment, you will see – and know through an inner knowing that is beyond doubt – that my life outlines a path that you too can follow until you win your ascension in the light. After you recognize the validity of that path, you can begin to move along that path more quickly than ever before.

It is my hope that my true teachings can reach a sufficient number of people who are ready at inner levels to embrace the true inner path that leads to the resurrection and the ascension.

This is indeed one of the main purposes behind the original Easter events. May my true teachings be resurrected in your heart, and may your Conscious You be resurrected and follow in my footsteps until I can greet you as you enter our Father's kingdom.

You often say that we need to become the Christ. In my experience, it is very difficult for people to accept that they are the Christ. For most people, the thought of declaring – even to themselves – that "I am the Christ!" is very frightening. How can people overcome that fear?

There are two main reasons why it is difficult for people to accept their Christhood:

• Outer pressure generated by the false prophets of this world. These are the prophets who have built the cult of idolatry around the outer person of Jesus Christ, saying that I was the only Son of God and the only one who could manifest Christhood. These false prophets have built an immense force, an immense beast, that has been running rampant in this world for 2,000 years, and actually for a lot longer. This force attacks people at the mental and emotional levels and makes it very difficult for them to accept the idea that they too are sons and daughters of God who have the potential to manifest Christhood and do the works that I did (John 14:12).

• The inner cause, namely a mechanism in human psychology. That cause is the person's human ego, or dweller on the threshold. This false self acts as an inner force, an inner beast, which attacks the Conscious You and seeks to make the Conscious You think and feel that it does not have the supreme self-worth that comes from accepting that you are a son or daughter of God.

(X)

Another aspect of this inner cause is that when you recognize that you have the potential to manifest Christhood, you also recognize that your entire life and your entire outlook on life needs to change. For many people this would mean a complete turnaround in the way they look at themselves and the way they look at life. It would also mean that people have to make dramatic changes in how they live their lives. Because the pseudo self is always reluctant to make changes, it clings to what is familiar. Even if what is familiar leads to suffering, people are reluctant to make a complete turnaround in their beliefs and lifestyle.

That is why the false prophets are so successful in selling people the dream of an outer, automatic road to salvation. It is so tempting for people to believe that by declaring me as their Lord and Savior, they can be saved without truly having to change themselves. In reality, the pressures from the outer enemies and the inner enemies are so great that it would be unrealistic to expect that anyone could instantaneously overcome them. That is why I stress the importance of following a gradual path. You have to start at your present level of consciousness and use the tools I give to gradually raise yourself until you can finally begin to accept your Christhood. There simply is no shortcut, there is no instantaneous solution, there is no magic wand that can instantly turn people into Christed beings.

It is correct that the underlying cause is fear, and as some modern psychologists are beginning to realize, there are only two basic emotions, namely love and fear. You want to get close to what you love, you want to attain union with what you love. You want to get away from what you fear, you want to attain separation from what you fear. There are lifestreams who have rebelled against God's law and God's will for this universe. This rebellion started with a being named Lucifer and spread to many other lifestreams who followed him when he fell in a previous sphere. The goal of Lucifer was to remove himself from God and create a world in which God is not found.

Lucifer's followers are still trying to get as far away from God as possible, and this proves that they are motivated by fear. This desire to get away from God is also influenced by many of the feelings that originate in fear, such as pride and anger. Nevertheless, fear, or the sense of separation, the desire to get away from God, is the primal emotion from which all negative human emotions originate.

The last 2,000 years represented an age in which people were meant to see and accept themselves as sons and daughters of God. During these past 2,000 years, the fear of being the Christ, or the fear of encountering the Christ, has been the predominant fear on this planet.

Is love the key to overcoming this fear? After all, the Bible talks about the perfect love that casts out fear (1John 4:18).

The all-important lesson that I am trying to get across in this book is that once you have descended into and become trapped by the death consciousness, you cannot use that state of consciousness to free yourself. You cannot solve a problem from the same state of consciousness that created the problem. You need an outer savior who can show you the path, the inner path whereby you can gradually regain contact with the inner savior of your Christ self.

The key to overcoming fear is love, however it is not human love. Human love cannot overcome fear. What can overcome fear is perfect love, namely the unconditional love of God. You can receive and experience that love only through your Christ self or through an outer teacher who has attained union with his or her Christ self. This explains why there is no instantaneous salvation and no instantaneous process for obtaining Christhood. What prevents you from experiencing the perfect love of God are the false beliefs, the psychological wounds, and the toxic energies that have accumulated in your energy field. In order to start the path that leads to Christhood, you must begin by doing the hard work of removing and resolving these obstacles.

As a visual illustration, imagine that your consciousness is a kaleidoscope. Throughout your many embodiments in the dense state of consciousness that has dominated this planet for thousands of years, you have accepted many false beliefs, received many psychological wounds and generated some misqualified energy. This would be comparable to putting pieces of colored glass into the kaleidoscope of self. When too many pieces of glass have accumulated in the kaleidoscope, the pure light of God cannot shine through to your conscious mind. You cannot experience the unconditional love of God, which truly rains upon the just and unjust. This love is always available to you, but you either do not see it or you cannot accept that you are worthy to receive it.

The only way to break the stalemate is to systematically start removing the colored pieces of glass in the kaleidoscope of self. As you clear away the debris, you will gradually begin to experience the unconditional love of God, and as this love shines into your consciousness, the darkness of fear will naturally disappear. The way to experience love and overcome fear is to clear your consciousness so that the unconditional love of God can flow through you. You cannot produce love with the lower mind. You can allow your mind to be a conduit through which the love of God can flow into this world.

You have described how, as we climb the spiritual path, we gradually clear away the obstacles that prevent us from accepting our Christhood. You have also said the path is not mechanical so what is the final step we need to take in order to manifest our Christhood?

Make a decision. Everything revolves around your free will so Christhood is not an automatic consequence of mechanically removing obstacles. Until you remove a sufficient amount of obstacles, you don't have the option to accept your Christhood. In the here and now, you are who you think you are so to be the Christ, you must stop thinking you are less than the Christ. Even when you have removed enough obstacles, you still have to make the decision to accept and affirm that you are the Living Christ on earth. You have to be willing to stand in front of the mirror and affirm: "I choose to be one with my God, and therefore I am the Living Christ in action here!"

You cannot make this decision before you have removed some of the obstacles to Christhood. However, you need to make that decision even though some parts of your subconscious mind cannot necessarily accept it. As you rise to higher levels of the path, you need to be alert to the signals from your Christ self, and when you get those signals, you need to consciously decide to accept and affirm your Christhood. When you do so, the forces of this world will come to you and seek to intimidate or tempt you into denying your Christhood. You need to anticipate this and keep affirming your Christhood until every part of your being accepts it. At that point, the prince of this world has nothing in you, and you will be who you really are instead of whom your ego or the world thinks you are. At that moment, you will be here below all that you are Above.

Some Christian mystics have talked about the dark night of the soul. Is that similar to what you experienced on the cross and how does it relate to building our identity as spiritual beings?

The dark night of the soul is indeed similar to what I experienced on the cross, but it does not have to happen during a dramatic event. Many spiritual seekers actually go through this initiation in their daily lives without realizing what is happening to them. The dark night can happen so gradually that people do not notice the shift represented by the dark night. To understand the dark night, you need to realize what I have said before, namely that the ultimate goal of the spiritual path is for you to become whole, to become the spiritual being here on earth that you already are in Heaven. You need to become spiritually self-sufficient so that you become a sun who is radiating God's light from within yourself. You no longer feel you are incomplete or that you need anything from outside yourself to be whole or to be who you are.

This is a very dramatic shift in consciousness and sense of identity compared to the ego-centered frame of mind that most people experience before they start the path. It can be fully understood only by contemplating a statement from the Old Testament that I referred to when the Jews wanted to stone me for blasphemy: "Jesus answered them, Is it not written in your law, I said, Ye are gods?" (John 10:34). As I have explained throughout this book, your true identity is that you are an individualization of God. You have full access to the infinite power of God, and the key to accessing that power is found inside yourself. The ultimate goal of the spiritual path is to bring you to the point where you can fully accept your identity as an individualization of God. To reach that state, you need to overcome all sense of being separated from God, all sense that you are incomplete or that you need anything from outside yourself. Because the kingdom of God is within you, you need nothing but that inner kingdom!

This is a subtle distinction so contemplate my words carefully. As I have said, at the level of the soul, you are who you think you are. You have created a sense of identity as not being God, as being separated from God and as being incomplete and unwhole. You have defined a set of limitations for who you are and what you can and cannot do. In reality, you are God and you have the power of God within you, meaning that there are no limitations. The only factor that limits you is the limitations you accept in your own mind. That is why I constantly told people that if they had faith – meaning oneness with the God within them – they could move mountains (Matthew 17:20) and do the things that I did (John 14:12). The reason being that God would be acting through them as he did through me.

To help you overcome this false identity, the ascended masters have created the concept of the spiritual path as a gradual and systematic road to spiritual growth. The path is very helpful for people at the lower levels of consciousness. As you come closer to full Christ consciousness, the concept of a path can become a trap because it implies a distance between where you are and where you need to go. As long as you think you are walking toward a goal, you obviously have not arrived, and you will never arrive as long as you see a distance between yourself and your destination. At the higher levels of the path, you need to abandon the concept of a path and leave behind all sense of separation between yourself and God.

This can be a very difficult challenge for people if they do not understand the teachings I have given in these books. It has caused many seekers to go into a blind alley because – for various reasons – they do not make that final decision to become whole and self-sufficient. Imagine the process followed by most lifestreams. They descend into the death consciousness and feel alone and abandoned by God. At some point, they turn around and reach for God, and the teacher appears. As they walk the spiritual path, they gradually raise their consciousness and make contact with their Christ selves and with their spiritual teachers. They realize they have not been abandoned by God and that we are here for them. They gradually come to rely more and more on help and direction from Above. They build their faith in God, but they see God as being outside themselves.

This faith in an external God is very valuable for the lifestream at a certain level of the path, but it cannot take the Conscious You all the way to complete self-sufficiency. Even though we are the spiritual teachers of a lifestream, we cannot take that Conscious You to the final breakthrough of realizing that it has everything from within itself. We can take a Conscious You right up to the point of facing the final initiation, but we cannot make the Conscious You take the final step into the inner light. The kingdom of God is within you, and you must enter it on your own.

Because we are true spiritual teachers, we have no desire to see people become codependent upon us. We want people to become independent. As the Conscious You rises to the higher levels of the path, we must and we will withdraw our support from it. We must wean the Conscious You from leaning upon us because, in the end, the Conscious You must lean on nothing beside itself, its own sense of identity. Your spiritual teachers are still outside yourself so as long as you think you cannot be whole without us, you will not be whole. This also holds true for your Christ self and — which is the hardest part to understand — even for God and your I AM Presence— if you see God or your I AM Presence as being separated from you. Any mental image that portrays God as being outside of or apart from yourself is a graven image that violates the first two commandments. You must come to a point where you dare to be who you are without leaning on support from any outside source.

As the Conscious You rises toward the final initiation, we will gradually withdraw our support from that person, and for some this can be quite a shock. People feel distraught, as I did on the cross. Although we start out gently by withdrawing only a small portion of our support and guidance, some people refuse to take the next step toward self-sufficiency, and they can become stuck at that level of the path and keep looking for the teacher or God outside themselves.

The enigma here is that the Conscious You has become used to relying on help from Above, yet it now needs to go within itself and no longer look to any outside source. If it does not go within itself, it will feel abandoned or stuck, and this feeling will persist until the Conscious You resolves the enigma. The problem is that we cannot help the Conscious You resolve this dilemma because the Conscious You needs to do so by using its own faculties. The Conscious You needs to win its own victory by using the power of God within itself instead of seeking power from an external source. The goal of the path is that the Conscious You finds God, but you can find God only in one place, namely the kingdom of God that is within you. As long as you look outside yourself, you will not find God!

No teacher can do this for you; you must do it yourself by finally deciding to simply be who you are in God. You must stop doing and simply be who you are as a God-free being. When the Conscious You resolves this enigma, it can give up the ghost (Mark 15:37) of the human ego and step into the light of God that now shines through the Conscious You from within itself. The Conscious You is no longer a moon reflecting the light of the I AM Presence; it is a self-sufficient sun that radiates the light of God in this world. It is now the light of the world (John 8:12). Therefore, I say to you: "Be the light of the world!"

This raises a question I have been pondering but never quite knew how to put into words. Who exactly am I? I mean, I understand I am not the human ego and that I need to leave this false sense of identity behind. I understand that I need to identify with the I AM Presence, but who or what is it that can identify itself with anything and that has the potential to become self-sufficient? Exactly what is the core of my being, my identity?

One might say that the core of your identity, the core of who you are, is your sense of self, your sense of who you are. Even though I have said that your God-given individuality is anchored in your I AM Presence, the core of who you are is anchored in the Conscious You as your sense of self. As I said, in the here and now – meaning at the level of the soul – you are who you think you are.

You must understand that the reason you find it difficult to formulate this question is that words are linear and the answer is not linear. As one possible explanation, we might say that at the very core of your being is a spark of identity, a divine spark. This is what we – for want of better words – call the Conscious You and it gives you the ability to know that you exist and decide who you are, who you want to be. This is your divine potential, and it is an individualization of God because God – at the very core – is self-consciousness, self-awareness. You can call it the self, the Conscious You, the divine ego, the superego, the I or anything else you like—as long as you don't think that it can be confined to words.

In the beginning was only God and God was whole and complete in itself. But God also is the drive to create, the drive to be more than it is. Out of that drive to be more – which is actually unconditional love – the entire world of form was created. As the Creator began to create this world of form, it decided that it wanted to experience and create the world from the inside as well as from the outside. The self-sufficient Being of the Creator created two individualizations of itself, two self-conscious beings, inside the world of form. Those beings embody the two basic polarities that the Creator used to create the universe. These two beings have also created extensions of themselves that can experience and co-create. This process was repeated innumerable times through the layers of vibration that make up the world of form. This has created a hierarchy of self-conscious beings reaching from God to you.

What drives everything in creation is the unconditional love that desires to be more of itself. When a self-conscious being is created, it is not whole and complete in itself. The first part of the being's journey is to attain this wholeness. Attaining wholeness means that you resolve the enigma of individuality, meaning that you decide who you are as an individual being while recognizing that you are part of the whole. You acknowledge your place in God's Being, you become self-sufficient in letting God's light shine through you from inside yourself.

When a self-conscious being has attained wholeness, it is filled with the desire to be more so it creates an extension of itself. When your divine parents attained wholeness, they desired to be more, and they created your I AM Presence as an individualization of themselves that is different from, more than, the sum of their parts. Your I AM Presence decided to be more, and it created an extension of itself that became your Conscious You. The Conscious You also has the seed of self-awareness within it, and your immediate task is to attain wholeness and become self-sufficient, self-luminous. At that point, you have magnified God within you and both your I AM Presence, and the entire hierarchy of self-aware beings from which you descend, become more. Even God in the highest sense becomes more through you. You have then won your immortality, but the journey doesn't stop there. You can now build on your immortal identity and become more than you were created to be.

To make a long story short, you are a spark of self-aware-ness – a spark of God's consciousness and Being – that has the ability to build a complete and self-contained sense of identity. It is up to you to build your identity as you choose. You have the potential to identify yourself as a God-free being who is part of God's magnificent creation, God's infinite desire to be more through you.

You have the unlimited creative potential to help God co-create the world of form and make that world more than even your Creator could imagine. The question really is: "What do you want to be in the present now, and what do you want to be in the eternal now?"

When there is no difference between who you are in the eternal now and who you are in the present now, you are being the more, you are being God in action where you are. You then become the open door that no human can shut, and when a critical mass of lifestreams attain this spiritual mastery, God will bring his kingdom into manifestation on earth. He will do so through his sons and daughters who have now become himself in form. They know they are God's and they know they are Gods.

14 | AS ABOVE, SO BELOW

You have talked about the ascended masters and that you are our spiritual teachers. What exactly do you want people to know about you?

I first of all want people to know that we exist and that we are here for them. When you ascend to the spiritual realm, you overcome all ego-centered, human motivation. We are here for one reason only, namely that we love God, we love our unascended brothers and sisters and we love planet earth. We have an unconditional love for each human being, and we have an uncompromising commitment to the spiritual growth of each lifestream. As a group, we are working to raise every lifestream and to manifest God's kingdom on earth. Beyond that, each person on earth has an ascended master assigned as his or her personal teacher and guide. This personal teacher is absolutely committed to your growth and is always ready to give you instructions and directions—if you will ask with an open mind and heart.

We want people to know that by sharpening their intuition and opening their minds and hearts, they will eventually establish a direct connection to their spiritual teachers. This will allow them to receive direct instructions for how they can fulfill the purpose for which they came to earth, how they can fulfill their divine plans. Our hope is to see the formation of a body of people on this planet, the Body of God on earth, in which each person is consciously connected to his or her Christ self and personal master. Through that vertical connection, people can then establish a horizontal connection between them, and thereby they can form a community, a movement, that can be our hands and feet on earth. This movement can then be instrumental in removing darkness from the earth and bringing God's kingdom into full manifestation on this planet.

I also want people to know that despite the seemingly chaotic conditions on earth, we of the ascended masters have a plan for a systematic improvement of life, the ascension of all lifestreams and the purification of the planet. We have a plan for bringing God's kingdom to earth and for establishing a golden age of freedom, peace, abundance and equal opportunity for all. This is no fantasy or utopian daydream. It is already a reality in the etheric realm, and it can be brought down into the material frequency spectrum within a matter of decades. However, we need a critical mass of people who can and will understand the equation of free will. As I have explained throughout this book, the basic law of this universe is the Law of Free Will. We of the ascended masters are fully capable of removing all darkness from the earth, and we can bring forth the ideas that are needed to establish a permanent golden age. The Law of Free Will does not allow us to act directly on earth, and the reason is that we are no longer in embodiment on this planet. The Law of Free Will mandates that only those who are in a physical body can act directly on planet earth.

As Shakespeare said: "All the world's a stage," and we of the ascended masters are no longer on stage. We cannot directly influence whether the play will have a happy ending. Only those who are on the stage of life on planet earth can give the drama a happy ending. However, we of the ascended masters can act as directors from outside the stage by giving ideas and guidance to our unascended brothers and sisters. For this to happen, a critical mass of people need to follow the path to personal Christhood and establish a direct connection to their Christ selves and to us. Thereby, we can and will bring forth the ideas as well as the spiritual light that is necessary to remove darkness from the earth and manifest a golden age.

I want people to know that there are currently millions of lifestreams who volunteered to come into embodiment at this critical time in the history of planet earth. They are here because they also have a deep love for God, other people and the earth. They wanted to be in embodiment at this critical time in order to help bring the golden age into manifestation. They have a deep longing to see God's kingdom manifest on earth, and they also have an intuitive sense of what God's kingdom is like and what it will take to bring it forth.

Unfortunately, many of these lifestreams have been trapped by the lies and the culture of anti-christ that has been deliberately designed by dark forces to prevent such lifestreams from manifesting their Christhood and walking the earth as the Living Christs in embodiment. Consider how much trouble I personally caused the dark forces on this planet. The last thing they want is for thousands of other people to walk the earth in the fullness of their personal Christhood, and they will do anything in their power to prevent this from happening.

As I explain in *The Mystical Teachings of Jesus*, there are currently 10,000 lifestreams in embodiment who have the potential to manifest their full Christhood in this lifetime. There are millions more who can manifest a high degree of Christhood in this lifetime. If the earth is to manifest a golden age, it is absolutely critical that these people are awakened to the existence of the spiritual path, to their Christ potential and to the potential for bringing the golden age into manifestation within the next few decades.

There is a great need for people to manifest their Christhood and build the golden age and the golden age consciousness. The true hope that we have for bringing out these teachings is to reach the people who took a vow to help bring the golden age to earth. They took this vow before their lifestreams came into embodiment and lost the memory of their divine plans. We hope to awaken the inner memory so these people can begin to consciously fulfill the roles they vowed to play before they entered the drama that we call planet earth.

I also want people to know that we of the ascended masters are not sitting passively by, waiting for people to awaken. In every age there have been a few people who have been awakened to the spiritual path and their potential to put on the mind of Christ. Through such people we have been able to bring forth teachings and techniques that people can use to transform their own lives and transform the planet. The release of new teachings has been greatly accelerated over the past century. We have sponsored several organizations and individuals through which we have brought forth new spiritual teachings in the form of progressive revelation. We have also brought forth new spiritual techniques for the transformation of toxic energies, as I have mentioned throughout this book. I want people to know that we have not stopped talking to our unascended brothers and sisters and that we will never do so. We of the ascended masters are eternally committed to bringing forth progressive revelation as the consciousness of humankind is being raised. We can tell people so much more today than we could tell them 2,000 years ago or even a decade ago.

We want people to understand that you are living at a very exciting time. The earth is in the process of making a transition from one spiritual age, often called the Age of Pisces, into the next spiritual cycle, called the Age of Aquarius. This is an exciting time because there is an extraordinary release of spiritual light from Above, and this gives people an unprecedented opportunity for spiritual growth. The importance of this is that the consciousness of humankind is being raised very rapidly, and this opens the door for the ascended masters to bring forth new spiritual teachings in the form of progressive revelation. Since the new millennium there has been a very significant raising of the planetary consciousness, and this is indeed why we have brought forth the websites and the books. This is a very significant dispensation for planet earth, and I hope many people will find these teachings and make use of them. By using these tools, people can truly accelerate the removal of darkness so we can enter a golden age with a minimum amount of upheaval in society and the natural environment.

I can witness to the fact that many lifestreams have this inner longing to play a part in bringing forth a golden age. It took me some time to consciously recognize this desire, but after I became aware of it, I realized that I had always had this longing. I have met many people who have had similar experiences, and I believe there are many people who have not yet been awakened. What can those who are awakened do to help bring in the golden age?

As I said, they can begin by realizing the equation of free will. We of the ascended masters have the power, the wisdom and the love to remove all darkness from the earth and bring in the golden age. We do not have the authority to act directly on planet earth. People in embodiment do not have the power to remove the darkness, but they do have the authority to act on this planet. The ascended masters cannot bring the golden age on our own and neither can our unascended brothers and sisters. The golden age can be brought only when there is cooperation, a figure-eight flow, a true sense of oneness, between the ascended masters and our unascended brothers and sisters. For there to be a golden age, we must establish oneness between Heaven and earth so that the perfection of God can be manifest below as it is already manifest Above.

The most important step in this direction is that a critical mass of people sincerely apply themselves to the spiritual path and as quickly as possible move toward the fullness of their personal Christhood. To this end, I strongly encourage people to apply the teachings and tools I have described in these books. I strongly encourage people to select a spiritual ritual and to give it faithfully. I strongly encourage them to work on establishing and strengthening their intuition and establishing a conscious contact to their Christ selves and through that to their spiritual teachers. As people begin to establish their personal connections, they will receive inner directions as to what they can personally do to bring forth the golden age.

It is extremely important that people get their own directions from within because only then will these directions be fully internalized. Only directions that are truly internalized can be acted upon with full strength. Over the millennia, we have seen so many people who became awakened to the need to save the earth, but they approached this task with a human motivation to do something important, to buy their salvation or to be thought wise among men. These people then used the outer mind, the human intellect, to decide what needed to be done. Their efforts did not have the true power that only comes from the mind of God, and they did not have the true vision that only comes from the mind of Christ. Neither were they motivated by unconditional love. As a result, these people's efforts fell by the wayside or created conflicts between groups of people who all thought they had the only possible solution to humankind's problems.

This is a pattern that we simply must overcome in this day and age, and it can be done only by each person establishing a vertical connection so that he or she can reach the ascended masters and get instructions directly from us. We are the command center, and we have a unified plan and vision. We are willing to work with millions of people on this planet, people who do not need to be horizontally connected through one central organization or religion. We prefer to work with individuals and groups who might not be connected on earth but who are still connected vertically to the ascended masters. We can then direct people from Above so that they pull in the same direction, even if they are not directly connected or even consciously aware that they are working for the same greater cause.

In the past, we have seen how a centralized organization can be taken over by the power elite, who begin to use that religion to control the population and prevent them from reaching their Christhood. This is the last thing we want to see happen in this age, and therefore we will not give full authority to one organization. Instead, we will give our sponsorship to individuals as they merit that sponsorship.

Obviously, we would like to see many individuals reach a high degree of Christhood and then come together to form communities, organizations and movements who can work to improve specific conditions on earth. We would even like to see these organizations be linked in a loosely-knit network that is not controlled by a central authority on earth but is under the command of the authority of the ascended masters. Here are some concrete suggestions for what people can do to help bring forth a golden age:

- Select and faithfully perform a ritual. Study some of the spiritual techniques that we have released over the past century, determine which ones appeal to you and then use them faithfully. It has a great impact when people come together and give such rituals in groups. One person giving decrees or invocations is powerful, but dozens or hundreds of people giving them together in the same location, or even at the same time over the Internet, has a much greater power. The effect of the work is multiplied exponentially with the number of people giving it together. This holds true for any other spiritual ritual. The true significance of a suitable ritual is that when you give it, you give the ascended masters the authority to act on earth. Many of our decrees and invocations give us the authority to remove the types of imperfect energies and dark forces mentioned in the rituals. We can step through the veil and act on earth through such rituals. The rituals combine the power of the ascended masters with the authority of our una-scended brothers and sisters.

- Tell other people about the existence of the spir-itual path and its importance for your life. Tell them about the universal spiritual path, but do not fall into the trap of seeking to convert them to a particular belief system or organization. In the past, so many people have attempted to convert everyone to one particular religion. What will truly change conditions on earth is that people follow the universal path, and they can do so by being a member of any spiritual or religious organization—or no organization. The true need of the hour is to make people aware of the universal path instead of spending your energy on converting them to a particular religion or organization.

• Take a stand for truth in whatever area of life is close to your heart. As I explain throughout this book, every area of life on this planet is infiltrated and affected by the lies spread by the forces of anti-christ. There is a great need for people who have the love and the drive to improve conditions in a particular area of life and who will make themselves experts in that field. Along with acquiring this expertise, these people need to establish the vertical connection to their Christ selves and the ascended masters. We will then give people the directions and ideas they need in order to expose the lie and bring forth truth in their particular area of expertise.

• Become the open door for bringing forth new ideas to improve life on earth. Many human beings have an unrealistic view of what has produced progress on this planet. They actually believe that human beings have come up with the science, the technology and the ideas that drive progress. In reality, most of the ideas that have brought progress to this planet have been inspired directly from the ascended masters. The people who brought forth these ideas were simply conduits, and they received these ideas from us because they had established a certain sensitivity of mind and heart. We have many more ideas that we long to bring forth, and we are willing to work with anyone who has a reasonably pure motive and an open mind and heart. We need those who are willing to make the effort to establish a connection to their Christ selves so they can become the open doors for bringing new ideas to this planet. We need those who are willing to purify their vision so they can see what the ideal society is like. People can perform a major service by steadfastly holding that immaculate vision for the earth.

• Be the light of the world. As I said: "As long as I am in the world, I am the light of the world" (John 9:5). When a person attains a high degree of Christhood, he or she becomes the open door for the light and the love of God to stream into this world. It is this light that will transform the world and replace the darkness. What is the key to being the light of the world? Once again, consider my saying: "The light of the body is the eye: if therefore thine eye be single, thy whole body shall be full of light" (Matthew 6:22). When you overcome duality, your whole body – meaning all of your four lower bodies – are filled with light, and then: "Ye are the light of the world. A city that is set on an hill cannot be hid" (Matthew 65:14). That is what I desire to see for all of the millions of people who have the potential to manifest a high degree of Christhood in this lifetime. By allowing God's light to flow through you, you can do more to bring the golden age than in any other way. It is by being the light of the world instead of doing with the outer mind that you can help save the world.

• We also have a great need to bring forth new spiritual teachings, and to do that we need those who are willing to be the open doors for these teachings. It is important for such people to understand that the new teachings we want to bring forth will not come in the form of fixed doctrines. We need those who are willing to look beyond the orthodox doctrines of the world's religions and bring forth new teachings in the form of the Living Word. The Living Word is not simply words that can be written down or spoken. The Living Word carries the vibration of truth and the power to raise people's consciousness. We have a great need for those who are willing to go through the rigorous training process of making themselves the open doors for the delivery of the Living Word. This entire book is indeed an example of the delivery of the Living Word, and there is far more in this book than the words printed on the page. These words carry a vibration that sensitive lifestreams will recognize. It is this vibration that has the power to awaken people from their spiritual sleep and transform their consciousness. We need many more people who can deliver the Living Word, and we are willing to release courses and establish a school for training people to deliver the Living Word. It was my hope that Christianity would become a movement based on the delivery of the Living Word. This did come to pass in the first decades of the Christian dispensation, but alas the Living Word was lost when the orthodox church started to form. This church replaced the Living Word with a dead doctrine, it replaced the spirit of the law with the letter of the law (2 Corinthians 3:6). It is high time to reestablish the spirit of the law, and I am calling for those who know, deep within their lifestreams, that they have the potential to be the instruments for the delivery of the Living Word.

•   As already mentioned, we have a great need for those who will form communities and movements to help bring forth the golden age consciousness and the golden age ideas in a particular area of life. We also have a great need for those who are willing to bring forth the universal teachings about the spiritual path that transcend all outer religions. We have a great need for those who will work on unifying the world's religions by demonstrating the universal path that unites them. We also need people to work on unifying science and religion and unifying all spiritually minded people on this planet. Our true goal is to see the formation of the one Body of God on earth, meaning people who are dedicated to the manifestation of the golden age and the establishment of their individual connections to their Christ selves. These people can form the Body of God on earth, which can act as the extension of the Body of God in Heaven, namely the ascended masters. We have a need for those who are willing to be here below all that we are Above.

You talk about organizations that have been sponsored by the ascended masters over the past century. According to what you are saying, these organizations were started for the specific purpose of bringing forth progressive revelation, and they each did so for a period of time. It was the new revelation and not the outer organization that was important. If people are dedicated to the cause of the ascended masters, should they always be look-

**ing for the latest revelation or is it okay to remain
with a particular organization even if it is not bringing forth new revelations?**

The reality of the situation is that for millennia the ascended
masters were not allowed to give certain types of spiritual
knowledge to the general public. This was done because
humankind was still in such a low state of consciousness that
there was a grave risk that such knowledge would be misused
on a large scale. Such knowledge was taught only to people
who were the close disciples of a spiritual teacher, or it was
taught in secret societies. You will see that I taught the multitudes in parables and expounded all things to my disciples
(Matthew 13:34-35).

In the late 1800s, we received permission to release some of
this spiritual knowledge in books so that the knowledge would
now be available to anyone. Since then, we have released such
knowledge – or rather fragments of it – through a number
of individuals and organizations. Some of these organizations
have had a more formal sponsorship by one or several members of the ascended masters. The knowledge is freely available
in the etheric realm, and anyone who is able to raise his or her
consciousness to the etheric level can access the information
and become an open door for bringing it to the public.

Obviously, the purity of a person's consciousness and
motives has a major impact on how correct and useful
the information is that is coming through that person. As
explained before, some channelers tune in to the emotional
(astral) or mental realm and receive information that is partially
erroneous or incomplete. We have sponsored several individuals and organizations in an attempt to give people the most
reliable information possible. Even our sponsorship is subject
to the free will of the messenger who is bringing forth the

information, and there is no guarantee that a messenger cannot color the information. For that reason, we have never given a monopoly to any messenger or organization, and we will never do so.

If you look at history, you will see that one of the major problems in the religious life of earth is that the relativity of the death consciousness gives rise to the idea that there can be only one true religion. I expose the fallacy of this belief in *The Mystical Teachings of Jesus.* Because the ascended masters are well aware of this problem, we do not grant exclusive rights to any organization. We have a body of teachings that we want to release, and we simply cannot allow the future of the world to depend on a few people or on a single organization. When we sponsor a messenger and an organization, it is for the purpose of bringing forth a certain body of teachings. When that purpose has been fulfilled, we move on and start another organization to bring forth the next level of teachings. Furthermore, if the messenger or the members of an organization fall prey to the temptations of pride, and begin to believe their organization has a monopoly on the ascended masters, we simply move on and withdraw our sponsorship. This often goes unnoticed by the members, or even the messenger, of an organization.

Progressive revelation is an ongoing process that will not end in the foreseeable future. Our goal is to avoid having one religion become as dominant in the new age as for example the Catholic Church was in the middle ages. This is the main reason we have sponsored several organizations and why we will continue to work with several organizations and individuals.

As I said, all seekers need to be aware that there might come a point when a certain teaching has taken them as far as it can take them. When they receive such directions from their Christ selves, they should be willing to move on and find the next teaching. If they are not willing to do so, they essentially abort their progress. It is also possible that some people can transcend their approach to a particular teaching and thereby stay in a certain organization.

We have no desire to see the organizations we have sponsored disappear because they still have viable teachings that can be of value to seekers. However, we do have a desire to see all spiritual teachers and organizations overcome the need to feel that they are more important than others or that they have the only true religion. This belief is so obviously a product of the duality consciousness that no true spiritual teacher or seeker should be stuck in this illusion.

Can you give us an example of why progressive revelation is important?

If someone is a member of an organization that is no longer bringing forth progressive revelation, that person should be willing to study the next teaching we are bringing forth, even if that person stays with the previous organization. You need to realize that conditions on earth are changing very rapidly so if you are loyal to the cause of the ascended masters, you need to have our most current information. After all, are you loyal to an organization or guru on earth or are you loyal to your ascended brothers and sisters in Heaven? You cannot rely exclusively on information we brought forth a century or even a decade ago.

For example, in several previous organizations, we talked about the need for people to make their ascensions. At the time, that was the highest realistic goal, given humankind's level of consciousness. Since then, the planet has been raised considerably, and our focus is now on having people manifest their full Christhood while they are still on earth. As mentioned earlier, there are currently 10,000 people in embodiment who have the potential to manifest full Christhood in this lifetime and millions more can manifest a high degree of Christhood. It would be a tragedy if any of these people became stuck in an earlier teaching and therefore focused their attention on making their ascension, thinking they would not reach Christhood until they left this planet. I need these people to focus on manifesting their Christhood as soon as possible.

The true need of the hour is that we have thousands of people who manifest their Christhood because this will raise the consciousness of humankind more than any other factor. This is the true second coming of Christ, and it is the only thing that will truly bring a new and better age. That is why the new Golden Rule that is meant to guide humankind over the next 2,000 years is: "Be here below, all that you are Above."

15 | IS JESUS OBSOLETE?

I have met many people who are open to the spiritual path, yet they think Jesus Christ is obsolete. Some of them have seen through the shortcomings of orthodox Christianity and think you have no real spiritual message. Others are open to the progression of spiritual ages and see you as the main spiritual teacher for the previous Age of Pisces. Because we have now moved into the Age of Aquarius, they think you are no longer needed. What would you say to such people?

I fully understand why so many people reject me. I fully understand why so many people have given up on all religion because of their disappointment with orthodox Christianity. I fully understand why so many spiritual seekers and New Age people have given up on Christianity and reject anything related to Christianity. However, these people are throwing their own Christ children out with the dirty bath water of human power struggles. Regardless of how I have been portrayed by orthodox Christianity, the fact is that I am a universal spiritual teacher, and I have much to offer to the spiritual seekers of today.

It is important for all spiritual seekers to realize that there are certain cycles in the religious life, the spiritual evolution, of this planet. Each cycle, or age, lasts approximately 2,000 years, and during that time humankind is meant to grow to a new level of spiritual awareness. As an individual, you can gain a great advantage from understanding the current cycle and the opportunities for spiritual growth that it offers. This is especially true at this time because we are moving into a new cycle, the Age of Aquarius, that has unique opportunities for growth.

As you point out, many spiritually minded people accept the progression of spiritual cycles and realize that I was the spiritual hierarch for the Age of Pisces. They also realize that I am not the spiritual hierarch for the next 2,000-year cycle of Aquarius. However, let me assure you that I am not done with planet earth, as expressed in the following quote: "I am with you alway, even unto the end of the world" (Matthew 28:20). I still have much to offer to this planet, and people will clearly see this when they understand the progression of spiritual cycles.

Many spiritual seekers seem to have overlooked the fact that one spiritual cycle builds upon the previous cycle. The Age of Pisces was meant to set a solid foundation for the Age of Aquarius. If you are a sincere spiritual seeker, it should be obvious that the key to moving into the consciousness of Aquarius is to fully understand and internalize the consciousness of Pisces. If you attempt to skip the consciousness of the previous age, it is like building a house without a foundation.

Many people realize that the Age of Aquarius is an age of freedom, yet what is the key to freedom? The true freedom that people are meant to attain in the new age is spiritual freedom and independence. People are meant to become spiritually self-sufficient so they no longer need an outer, dogmatic religion but can fulfill the following prophecy: "But they shall sit every man under his vine and under his fig tree; and none shall make them afraid: for the mouth of the LORD of hosts hath spoken it" (Michah 4:4).

What is the key to spiritual freedom? I would hope I have made it clear that it is to rise above the duality of the death consciousness and attain Christ consciousness. Only by becoming free from the dualistic extremes of the death consciousness, can you win true spiritual freedom. You must go beyond the relative opposites that spring from the serpentine mind. One such extreme is the belief held by many Christians that you can be saved only be being a member of a Christian church. The opposite extreme is the belief held by many New Age people that you need to reject all organized religion and be a free agent, doing whatever feels good. Both of these extremes are based on a limited understanding of freedom.

The serpents of this world have found two main ways to pervert the concept of freedom. One is to seek to take freedom away through excessive control, and this is what you see outpictured in dogmatic religions and political tyrannies. The other way is to remove all restrictions and say that people can do whatever they want, as you see in some parts of the New Age movement and in some political philosophies. The problem with both approaches is that they deny the need for Christ discernment. One extreme says that people shouldn't think on their own because the church or the state will think for them. The other extreme says that people shouldn't think on their own because anything goes.

The key to freedom is to realize that because the universe will mirror back whatever you send out, you can be free only by being in harmony with the laws of God. Anything else will only hurt yourself and restrict your creative freedom. The true spiritual freedom that humanity is meant to attain in the Age of Aquarius can be obtained only through the Christ consciousness. The way to manifest Christ consciousness is to discover and internalize my true teachings about the inner path to Christhood.

I realize that this inner path has been completely perverted and obscured by orthodox Christianity. That is why I am now bringing forth new teachings to tell today's spiritual seekers about the true path. The reason is that until you follow that path and attain some degree of personal Christhood, you simply cannot move into the consciousness of the Aquarian age.

Many spiritual seekers are sincere about bringing a new age of spirituality. If these people truly want to help bring in this golden age, they need to realize that the new age will not come until they themselves have learned the lessons they were meant to learn during the Age of Pisces. Many people are open to new spiritual teachings yet reject me as being outdated. Why not look for new teachings about my true message so that you can fully learn the lessons of the Age of Pisces and build a solid foundation for entering the consciousness of Aquarius?

The progression from one age to the next is not something that happens automatically when you reach a certain date. It is more than anything else a transformation in consciousness. The earth will not move fully into the Age of Aquarius until a critical mass of people have manifested the Christ consciousness that they were meant to attain in the Age of Pisces. The problem right now is that this goal has not been met, and the planet is currently in a precarious position. The earth is wobbling between two states of consciousness, and this could potentially lead to upheaval in nature and society, as we explain in *Healing Mother Earth*.

Who will be willing to help us break this impasse? Those who are willing must take a serious look at my true teachings.

Because I was the main spiritual teacher sent to teach people about the path to Christhood, I am by no means obsolete in this age. Most of the more mature spiritual seekers could make an immense contribution to the growth of humankind by internalizing the teachings I have given in these books. If you look at the planet today, it should not be difficult to see that mainstream Christians are not likely to accept the teachings I give here. My best hope for quickly raising the planet into the Aquarian consciousness is the many people who have already discovered the spiritual path in one form or another. I need these people to realize that the need of the hour is personal Christhood and that nothing else will do.

The golden age will not come until a critical mass of people manifest individual Christhood. As mentioned, there are currently 10,000 people on planet earth who have manifested a high degree of personal Christhood at inner levels. Unfortunately, the vast majority of these people do not consciously recognize their inner attainment, and they do not dare to acknowledge and express it. There are also millions of people who have manifested a high degree of Christhood. These people could quickly make tremendous progress if they would consciously acknowledge their potential and be willing to engage in the path of expanding their Christhood.

Such people can be found in every walk of life. Many of them are found in traditional Christianity. Many of them are found in other religions. Many of them belong to no particular religion or subscribe to scientific materialism. A substantial portion of them are found in the New Age movement. I need these people to quickly come to a conscious realization of who they are and why they are here. I am constantly trying to reach out to all of these people. However, I do believe that the most receptive people should be those who have already discovered the spiritual path.

Many Christians use this quote to argue that you are the only road to Heaven: "I am the way, the truth, and the life: no man cometh unto the Father, but by me" (John 14:6). What is your response to that?

My response is that the orthodox interpretation of this statement is incorrect. As I explain in this book, membership of a Christian church will not automatically get you to Heaven. A more correct interpretation is to say that because I had attained oneness with the universal Christ mind, I was speaking on behalf of that mind. No one comes to the Father without putting on the mind of Christ. Nevertheless, the quote also has a deeper meaning.

When a spiritual age comes to a close, the spiritual hierarch for that age doesn't simply vanish. Instead, he or she is promoted to a higher position, and I have indeed been given a spiritual office as the Savior for all human beings. The consequence is that in order to permanently ascend to the spiritual realm, a lifestream must pass through my spiritual office and my Sacred Heart. This has certain consequences.

Because of my office, I cannot allow lifestreams to enter the spiritual realm until they have attained Christ consciousness. Doing so would compromise my assignment from God. Again, this does not mean that a person has to be a member of a Christian religion. But it does mean that the lifestream must choose to approach me and my office.

A lifestream simply cannot enter Heaven until it approaches me, and it cannot do so until it makes peace with me and everything I represent. That is another reason the teachings in these books and on my website [www.askrealjesus.com] are so crucial. There are currently millions of mature lifestreams who are being held back in their growth because they have come to accept a false image of me. These lifestreams could greatly speed up their progress by letting go of this image so they can accept me as a universal spiritual teacher, as their older brother, who is here to help them walk the path and attain Christ consciousness. I sincerely hope I can reach these people with my inner teachings. I am willing to make peace with every lifestream on earth. I hope every spiritual seeker is willing to make peace with me.

You have said that no teaching has a monopoly on truth and that no person or organization can give us everything we need to know about the path. I assume that holds true for these books and that people should not look at them as having everything they need. They should feel free to seek out other sources of information. Is that correct?

It is not my intent to give people everything there is to know about the spiritual path in one book. That simply wouldn't be possible, as the Bible demonstrates: "And there are also many other things which Jesus did, the which, if they should be written every one, I suppose that even the world itself could not contain the books that should be written" (John 21:25). I do indeed have much more to say about the spiritual path, and it is important to understand that the path can be described in many ways. This book is one way, but not the only way.

My goal for these books has been to give people everything they need to know in order to discover the spiritual path and anchor themselves firmly on the path. That goal has been accomplished because if people will make use of the tools I describe and internalize the insights I give, they will gradually establish a connection to their Christ selves. The real goal of my teachings is to connect you to your Christ self, and it will be highly beneficial to read the books many times to find the hidden gems that are easy to overlook.

Once you have established the connection to your Christ self, you will get personalized directions from within. This might include directions to study other spiritual teachings, or it might include direct revelations that go beyond any written teaching. In the end, there are certain spiritual mysteries that cannot be written down because they must be experienced directly. These books contains keys to unlocking the inner experience, but they can work only when people read the books with a certain level of sensitivity.

The most important thing people can understand about the spiritual path is that the key to following the path is not found in this – or any other – book. The key to the kingdom of God is found within yourself. There is only one path to God, and that is the inner path. At a certain level of the spiritual path, a person needs an outer teaching and it needs to follow that teaching. This is natural because the lifestream needs protection, direction and an anchor point. But at a higher level of the path, the lifestream needs to move beyond any outer teaching. The person needs to follow the true path of the ascended masters, which we have given on this planet for eons. The true path is:

- You study a teaching.

- You absorb the teaching.

- You become one with the teaching.

- You become one with the teacher.

- Then, you become the teacher. You become the next teacher who is witnessing to the truth of the path.

This is your calling. We of the ascended masters have sponsored many organizations to bring forth the true teachings on the inner path. But our goal has never been to create students who forever remain students and followers. Our goal has always been to raise you up to be the masters that you truly are and to be those masters while you are still on earth. The only teaching we have ever given is the teaching about the inner path. It has been expressed through many different outer teachings and churches and organizations. It has been expressed in many disguises. But there is only one teaching. There is only one truth. There is only one path. It is the inner path of becoming all that you are. Follow that path and be here below all that you are Above. This is the master key to manifesting God's kingdom on earth as it is already manifest in Heaven.

About the Author

Kim Michaels is an accomplished writer and author. He has conducted spiritual conferences and workshops in 14 countries, has counseled hundreds of spiritual students and has done numerous radio shows on spiritual topics. Kim has been on the spiritual path since 1976. He has studied a wide variety of spiritual teachings and practiced many techniques for raising consciousness. Since 2002 he has served as a messenger for Jesus and other ascended masters. He has brought forth extensive teachings about the mystical path, many of them available for free on his websites: *www.askrealjesus.com, www.ascendedmasteranswers.com, www.ascendedmasterlight.com* and *www.transcendencetoolbox.com.* For personal information, visit Kim at *www.KimMichaels.info.*

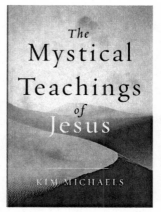

The teachings in this book have helped hundreds of thousands of people gain a deeper appreciation for Jesus's teachings about the mystical path that he taught 2,000 years ago and that he still teaches today—for those who are able to make an inner connection with him.

TODAY MANY PEOPLE CANNOT find a lasting heart connection to the real Jesus and his teachings because, according to most Christian churches, Jesus no longer talks to us. In reality, Jesus is a spiritual being and he is working to help all people who are able to raise their consciousness and attune to his Presence. For the past 2,000 years he has maintained a line of communication through those who have been willing to serve as messengers for his Living Word and who have pursued an understanding of his true message instead of settling for official Christian doctrines.

In this book, the ascended Jesus reveals the mystical teachings that he gave to his most advanced disciples. He explains why his true teachings are as relevant today as they were two millennia ago and how you can develop a personal relationship with him— one of the most remarkable spiritual teachers of all time.

Once you admit that mainstream religious traditions have not answered your questions about life, it is truly liberating to read the deep and meaningful answers in this book. Encouraging, moving and profound, this enlightening book will help you attain inner attunement with Jesus, even mystical union with him.

You will learn how to:
- recognize the silent, inner voice of Christ in your heart
- achieve permanent inner peace and happiness by getting connected with the Christ Consciousness
- heal yourself from emotional wounds
- get guidance from Jesus, who is your greatest teacher and friend
- communicate directly with Jesus

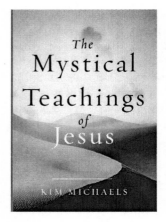

The *Mystical Teachings* of *Jesus*

KIM MICHAELS

The teachings in this book have helped hundreds of thousands of people gain a deeper appreciation for the mystical path that Jesus taught to his disciples 2000 years ago, the path towards union with God, a state of mind beyond most people's highest dreams.

TODAY MANY PEOPLE HAVE trouble discovering the small, easy and practical steps towards a state of consciousness that is beyond human conflicts and pitfalls. In this book the ascended master Jesus describes how to start walking the mystical path that will eventually restore our most natural ability: the direct experience of God within ourselves.

This book empowers you to discover your personal path and make steady progress towards peace of mind and an inner, mystical experience of God.

Inspiring and profound, this enlightening book contains questions and answers that are easy to read and that help you walk the mystical path of Jesus.

You will learn how to:

- Use the cosmic mirror to speed up your growth
- Get out of old reactionary patterns
- Become free from difficult situations and guilt
- Control your mind
- Leave behind a painful past
- Open your heart to the flow of love from within
- Heal the wounds in your psychology

CPSIA information can be obtained at www.ICGtesting.com
Printed in the USA
LVOW07s1708020915

452547LV00007B/998/P